Praise for **Exceptional Experiences**

"Neen brilliantly articulates what we have long championed at Ritz-Carlton—that exceptional service comes from genuine human connection, not extravagance. Her concept of systemized thoughtfulness provides an elegant framework for delivering consistent excellence that leaves lasting impressions on clients. This essential guide will help leaders across industries create the kind of memorable experiences that transform customers into passionate advocates for life."

Herve Humler, cofounder, The Ritz-Carlton Hotel Company

"*Exceptional Experiences* offers a fresh, fun take on how luxury brands can stand out from the pack and connect meaningfully with customers. Neen's energy and wit come alive through her storytelling—it's like hearing from a dear friend."

Tim Mapes, SVP and chief communications officer, Delta Air Lines

"Neen captures what makes luxury experiences exceptional—genuine human connection and attention to detail. Virtuoso Members and Partners have leveraged her principles to enhance their already successful practices. This book is a must-read for leaders who know that creating meaningful moments enhances our clients' Return on Life, an outcome of a successful Virtuoso relationship."

Matthew Upchurch, chairman and CEO, Virtuoso Travel

"Neen has written the book that every leader of a company, service professional, and all who care about client relationships, brand loyalty, and long-term referrals should read. *Exceptional Experiences* does more than define luxury—it reintroduces it as something deeply human. Through thoughtful interviews with those who deliver excellence every day, Neen proves that luxury is not about price—it is about how intentionally we treat others. She shows us how removing friction, anticipating needs, and paying attention meaningfully builds trust, loyalty, and reputation. Her model is practical and powerful—a system to create consistent, memorable moments that lead to stronger relationships, deeper connections, and what The Ritz-Carlton Leadership Center has called 'irrational loyalty.' What I take away is this: luxury is not something you buy, it is something you create. And when done well, it becomes the reason people come back—and the reason they tell others about you. If this is what you are looking for, then start here."
Caroline K. Huo, director, luxury division, Keller Williams Realty International

"Smart, simple, and implementable. Neen created a blueprint for leaders of any industry to define their differentiators through the large and (especially) the small details. This is the how-to for creating consistent, lasting impressions and supercharging brand value and impact."
Ebonne Leaphart, vice president, Comcast Experience Group

"Rethink what you know about luxury. It's not indulgence, it's being your best, and giving your best. Neen is your perfect guide to how to be exceptional and create extraordinary moments."
Michael Bungay Stanier, author, *The Coaching Habit*

For more toasts to *Exceptional Experiences*, flip to the back of the book!

FIVE LUXURY LEVERS

TO ELEVATE EVERY ASPECT

OF YOUR BUSINESS

Exceptional Experiences

| Neen James |

Exceptional Experiences

PAGE TWO

Copyright © 2025 by Neen James

All rights reserved. No part of this book may be reproduced, stored in a retrieval system or transmitted, in any form or by any means, without the prior written consent of the publisher or a license from The Canadian Copyright Licensing Agency (Access Copyright). For a copyright license, visit accesscopyright.ca or call toll free to 1-800-893-5777.

The Experience Elevation Model™ is a trademark owned by Neen James

Some names and identifying details have been changed to protect the privacy of individuals.

Cataloguing in publication information is available from Library and Archives Canada.
ISBN 978-1-77458-625-9 (hardcover)
ISBN 978-1-77458-626-6 (ebook)

Page Two
pagetwo.com

Page Two™ is a trademark owned by Page Two Strategies Inc., and is used under license by authorized licensees

Jacket and interior design by Peter Cocking
Illustrations by Jeff Winocur
Printed and bound in Canada by Friesens
Distributed in Canada by Raincoast Books
Distributed in the US and internationally by Macmillan

25 26 27 28 29   5 4 3 2 1

neenjames.com

To my beautiful mum,

You showed me that even in the toughest times, everyone deserves luxury. Thank you for role-modeling that luxury isn't about money, it's how we make others feel.

Because of you, I know everyone deserves to be seen, heard, and valued. You taught me that thoughtfulness is an everyday choice and true generosity comes from the heart.

Your wisdom and kindness are the foundation of everything I believe about creating exceptional experiences. I love you.

Contents

· · · · ·

Yes, Luxury Applies to You *1*

PART ONE **Luxury Is About Experiences, Not Things**

1 The Golden Key to Revenue *9*

2 Becoming Exceptional *27*

3 The Experience Elevation Model *43*

PART TWO **Five Luxury Levers**

4 Captivating Experience *59*

5 Demonstrating Experience *73*

6 Elevating Experience *99*

7 Inspiring Experience *117*

8 Leveraging Experience *127*

Keep Reaching for Luxury *149*

Grand Cru (A Fancy Name
for Acknowledgments) *155*

Sources of Exceptional Experiences *161*

Luxury is a meaningful human connection.

Cynthia Coutu
founder, Delectabulles

Yes, Luxury Applies to You

· · · · ·

Dearest gentle reader, you may not yet think that the word "luxury" applies to your brand, yet I am convinced that it does. Hear me out…

Many of us associate luxury with expensive things that money will buy. Let me show you that luxury is, in fact, about experiences you can offer—experiences that will engage your potential clients and delight your existing ones so that they choose to invest more with you. I realize the word "luxury" can be divisive; it means different things to different people. To me, luxury is about attention, and attention is about connection. So, in my mind, luxury is all about human connection. As a leader, you likely already know just how important that connection is to the success of your team, your organization, and your brand.

Luxury is in my DNA (despite my very humble beginnings). It is a daily commitment to excellence, where I prioritize attention to thoughtful details and, as a daily lifestyle, surround myself with beauty and comfort and order. It is being mindful of the big things as well. And yes, it is a little indulgent—but always for a good purpose. This is my personal ethos: Luxury is not an external attribute. It is a core element of my essence that shapes my actions, mindset, and approach to life and business. By the time you have finished reading this book, maybe it will be for you too.

Why do I think that? Because I believe to my core that luxury is about how you, your business, and your brand show up in the world as the most exceptional version of you. It's how you make people feel, how people experience YOU. In other words, I believe that luxury is, above all, an experience—one that anyone can create with just a few simple levers. Luxury begins with you, your personal brand, and the ways in which you personalize your connection with others, pay attention, act thoughtfully, and operate in the world. It is about your leadership. How you make others feel, the sensations and the memories of your leadership and your brand, will affect how people think of your organization and what they tell the world about you.

In any industry, applying luxury principles and systems is a golden key to your relationship with clients. In the following pages of this book, I have distilled the findings of original research I commissioned into luxury mindsets so that, together, we can explore practical (but still luxe)

Luxury isn't about money. It's about moments.

. . . . .

strategies for you to elevate your existing clients' experiences and attract new clients to your organization. I've also interviewed an impressive number of leaders of luxury businesses and brands and other organizations that cater to luxury clients. But most of all, I've worked for over twenty years distilling what I've found into five principles and practices that any business—and any individual—can apply. On this journey, we'll unlock how these five luxury levers come together in my proprietary Experience Elevation Model, and how you can use them and the luxury mindset they represent to differentiate your brand, increase revenue from existing clients, and transform your client relationships. Sound good?

Like any interesting journey you take (personally or professionally), integrating the principles of luxury requires effort—exceptional experiences don't just happen. If they did, everyone, including your competitors, would be providing them, and then the experiences would not be exceptional. Your results will be based on where you focus your attention. Being intentional about the amount of time and effort you invest in the planning and execution of your journey will accelerate your results. But even applying just a few of the systems of elevation presented in this book is likely to bring you an increase in revenue and client satisfaction, and maybe even your own.

Applying the principles of luxury (according to Neen) to your leadership style and to leading your brand, regardless of your title or industry, will also elevate everything you and your organization do. How do I know? Because hundreds of my clients around the world and thousands of my audience members have implemented these principles and systems, and they have seen those results. That's why I am excited to share them with you. I hope they inspire you to not only to influence your organization and better serve your clients, but also to notice how luxury, and particularly its quality of personalization and customization, improves your relationships with clients and colleagues in your commercial ecosystem.

When you reach the end of our journey together, you will have a contextual model (that's my fancy name for a framework) that guides you to build luxury systems to attract and retain the clients that you want to work with, and then invite those same clients to advocate for you and your brand. All this not only increases mind share (so you are top of mind for your clients and prospective clients), but also market share (because they sing your praises to other people you want to engage in your business). Isn't that what we all want? To have people advocate for us and our brands out in the world and create an even more exceptional world to work and play in?

Yes! Right, let's begin!

Making moments matter,

Neen

PART ONE

Luxury Is About Experiences, Not Things

1
The Golden Key to Revenue

· · · · ·

You are leading in extraordinary times. Differentiating your brand has never been more challenging, and yet, regardless of your industry, you can draw on the principles of luxury to create exceptional experiences that will set your brand apart.

*Luxury is about making people feel
seen, heard, and valued
through unforgettable experiences.*

Cornelia Samara
general manager and regional vice president,
Four Seasons Philadelphia

What if I told you that a widow saved the champagne industry? And not recently—two centuries ago.

At the tender age of twenty-seven, a young widow, Barbe-Nicole Ponsardin, found herself at the helm of her husband's champagne house, facing the challenges of running a business during Napoleon's reign and the upheaval of a war-torn Europe. Napoleon was stealing resources and attention, but despite these challenging times, Barbe-Nicole transformed the champagne industry and set the gold standard for true luxury and exclusivity. She became a wildly successful businesswoman living in a milieu where women did not have the right to vote or to a secondary school or university education.

This story may sound familiar to you because you have met the young widow from two centuries ago. You have seen her at important events, weddings, hotels, perhaps even in your grocery store. You have, I promise. You would recognize her by the distinct yellow label on her champagne bottle. Yes, I am speaking of Veuve Clicquot. (Let me teach you a word of French. *Veuve* is the French word for "widow.") Voilà! Barbe Nicole Ponsardin's married name was Madame Clicquot, and she became otherwise known as Veuve Clicquot.

In the world of luxury, where every detail is meticulously crafted to deliver an unparalleled experience, her name stands out as a beacon of excellence and resilience. She envisioned a champagne that was not just consumed, but feted—a symbol of celebration, excellence, and life itself. She didn't set out to create a luxury product, even though her champagne is synonymous with luxury today. Instead, she understood inherently that luxury is not just about a product, but about an experience.

Do not be mistaken, though; it was not easy for Madame Clicquot to execute her vision. The Napoleonic Wars had devastated the economy, and her wine business was on the brink of collapse. The vineyards suffered from harsh weather, workers needed to be paid, and supplies were dwindling. During a particularly tough time, she sold her possessions to maintain the livelihoods and loyalty of her workers, demonstrating that luxury leadership is as much about heart as it is about vision. This spirit of determination saw her through the darkest times, even when others doubted and challenged her. Where some might have succumbed to the pressures, Madam Clicquot rose to them. She examined every aspect of the champagne process and asked herself, "How could we improve this?"

Did you know that champagne used to be quite cloudy, with unsightly sediment in it? I sometimes imagine Madame Clicquot sitting there, perhaps a little annoyed that some sediment had stuck to her teeth. Not the experience she wanted. I see her wondering, "How do I improve this?" So she invented the riddling process. This method—known as *méthode traditionnelle* and still seen today in *champagne maisons* (just a quick warning, in addition to some new French terms, you will be learning some fabulous champagne terms as you read this book)—coaxes the sediment down the neck of the bottle, where it can then be removed. She discovered it because she had drilled holes in her dining table to store the bottles on an angle—genius! So she began to sell clear champagne while her competitors were still serving the cloudy varieties.

She used her desire for experience to inspire innovation. And this innovation alone revolutionized the industry.

Madame Clicquot's story is a testament to the luxury mindset created by the five luxury levers. It demonstrates the power of innovation, determination, and an unyielding commitment to excellence. The widow did not just create a product, she created a legacy. Her life and work embody the essence of luxury *experiences*—providing exceptional service and an unforgettable experience crafted with care, precision, and an eye for the extraordinary. In her case, it happened to produce a luxury product, as well.

Like Madame Clicquot, you are leading in extraordinary times. Never has the market been tougher, and never have the demands been fiercer to gain market share and drive revenue. It feels like there is never enough time. Finding the right talent is like finding the pot of gold at the end of the rainbow. Your competitors are doing everything they can to drown your business out. It can feel like a competition for who can yell the loudest over the most social channels. And despite all your efforts, not much seems to be working to set your business apart. Perhaps there is a better way—a way to differentiate your business and gain market share, not by yelling the loudest but, as Madame Clicquot did, by elevating every aspect of your business.

As a confidante to many CEOs of luxury and legacy brands across industries, I have countless conversations and coaching sessions about how my executive clients can increase revenue, differentiate their organizations, and build advocates (internally and externally). All my clients want to increase their mind share (which means to be top of their clients' minds) and market share (making shareholders and investors happy).

Chances are, you want that too, as a leader of a team, owner of a business, or a volunteer on a board. Or you might be someone who delivers experiences to clients, guests, or customers. Whatever your role, and regardless of where I am meeting you on your journey, you will find the strategies in this book apply to leading and delivering exceptional experiences—that is, applying luxury principles to all you do. When you provide exceptional experiences to your team and clients, you deepen relationships and you gain mind share. And when you gain mind share, you increase your revenue (market share).

Revenue reflects relationships—the stronger your client relationships, the higher the revenue. If you are at the top of your clients' minds when they want or need your product or service, they are more likely to invest in you and your business first.

My first full-time job out of high school was in a large corporate bank in Australia. I will never forget my scary boss; he was gruff and direct, but he shared a valuable lesson I have remembered my whole career: "It is easier to upsell an existing client than to attract a new one." Those words stuck with me, as I realized that you earn the most money from the clients who love you and want to return to you and refer others to you. Those are the kinds of relationships to invest time and attention into.

Luxury Is a Mindset

You might know that one of the books I authored is called *Attention Pays*. I've always believed that attention is about connection. *Attention Pays* outlines that an intention makes attention valuable. This new book, *Exceptional Experiences*, is the evolution of my attention work. The tendency in business is to think you must attract new clients, and that is true. But you need to pay more attention to your existing clients to generate new business with them. Like bubbles in a bottle of bubbly, they are already captured in your system. You just need to focus your time, attention, and energy on transforming them from clients into advocates.

As my work in attention evolved, I began to connect attention with luxury more and more, and eventually sought out research to explore my belief that luxury is a mindset. I have a long career in consulting in luxury industries, and while I intuitively sensed that luxury is a mindset, I could not just go into my clients boardrooms and say, "Luxury is a mindset, okay?" They needed to know what the evidence and data said. While there were many studies on how luxury makes people *feel*, that wasn't what I needed for my executives. Leaders like you would want to know how thinking with a luxury mindset gives your organizations more market share, right? That meant my research needed to uncover what people *think* about luxury, and how that thinking influenced their decisions to invest in luxury experiences. But guess what? There was no study in luxury mindset, not a single one. So I commissioned my own.

Working with the incredible Audience Audit team founded by the brilliant Susan Baier, we created the only study of its kind in the world—a proprietary research study into the mindsets that drive luxury purchases. For my clients and their teams, I wanted to clearly define what luxury is, its qualities. And I wanted to know who and what influences the decisions of the leaders my clients tend to cater to, how long it takes them to make a decision, what inspires them to buy, and how often they make purchases. I wondered: How does luxury impact their confidence? What messaging influences people's behaviors with a brand? How does luxury impact careers and reputations?

One fascinating finding of the study is that, based on their attitude about buying luxury products, services, and experiences, there are four different ways your customers and clients think about luxury:

- the reluctant and removed (people who find luxury is hard)
- the pro prioritizer (those who use luxury for their career and reputation)
- the confident and content (luxury isn't a priority for them)
- the luxury lover (who believes everyone deserves luxury every day)

Later chapters go into these types in more detail, and you can find an executive summary of the research on the Luxury Mindset website (luxuryisamindset.com).

Despite the differences between them, each luxury mindset agreed on two things: luxury is a reward for hard work, and luxury is more about experiences than things.

Even if you aren't in the luxury industry, knowing about the luxury mindsets is important for you and your team. You need to be able to appeal to the clients you want to attract by leveraging your messaging to them in all aspects of your business. Knowing the decision-making process and what appeals to each mindset helps you build the systems of elevation you need to provide exceptional experiences for them.

Luxury Is Inclusive and Exclusive

Before we go any further, allow me to share some of my own story with you.

Growing up, I didn't live a privileged life. I wasn't born with a silver spoon in my mouth. I didn't have what society might call a wealthy or luxurious upbringing—quite the opposite. When I was a little girl, I lived in a caravan (in America, they call it a trailer park). My single mum (yes, that's how we spell "mum" in Australia) raised two little girls by cleaning houses, picking lettuce, and selling fruit on the side of the road.

I was a happy and outgoing kid, and I also understood that my sister and I weren't like the other kids in our school. Those other kids had two parents, could afford to enjoy school trips, did extra sports activities outside school hours, learned piano and other musical instruments, took ballet lessons, and, after school breaks, shared where they'd been on holidays (some of you call them vacations). My family did not have the means to do any of those things. As a little girl, I appreciated Mum doing the best she could, even though I wanted what the other kids had, wanted to be part of the cool kids, and was teased for the clothes I wore, which were made with love and sometimes a little too big because they were hand-me-downs from a cousin.

But despite my humble beginnings, I got my love of luxury from Mum. She always wanted everything to feel special for those around her, especially my sister and me.

You don't need a luxury product to provide a luxury experience.

......

When we were little girls, Mum always ensured that we were surrounded by beauty. At the end of a busy shift, despite how tired she was, she would walk through a community garden and pick a flower. She would bring it home to our caravan and put it in a glass, which we called a vase because we felt fancy. This little act of everyday luxury brought more beauty into our lives, and it meant everything to us. My mum role-modeled for me that luxury is about experiences, about how to make people feel special and seen. She showed me that even without money, we all deserve luxury, every day.

In this way, luxury is exclusive *and* inclusive.

When I say "exclusive," I mean that luxury is about exceptional experiences that make you feel great, like a star on the red carpet. When I say "inclusive," I mean that luxury is for everyone, all the time, the way it was for my sister and me growing up.

But luxury isn't just about what's present—it's also about what's absent. When forms need filling (again), when bots interrupt your journey, when queues (lines for my American readers) snake endlessly, or when voicemails lead nowhere, you're experiencing the antithesis of luxury. It's the luggage you're forced to drag, the clutter that clouds your space, the chaos that drowns conversation, and the rudeness that ruins a pleasant moment. While sometimes we might struggle to define the perfect luxury experience, we instantly recognize its opposite: those friction-filled interactions that leave us frustrated, disappointed, and wondering why it had to be so hard. Those interactions are costing your business money. They are not leaving the impression that your brand is exceptional. True luxury eliminates these pain points, replacing them with seamless, thoughtful experiences that feel natural and extraordinary.

Luxury Transcends Industry

While consulting with the incredible Canadian executive team at Fairmont Hotels, I explored their definition of luxury and learned why they enjoy such a high level of return visits and praise from their guests. We identified that luxury is more than just high-end products or lavish services—it's a profound emotional experience, crafted through exclusivity, personalization, and lasting memories. Luxury transcends price tags or brand names. It is about creating a sense of well-being, where each guest feels valued and uniquely understood. From the softness of fine linens to the rare privilege of savoring one of only thirty-seven bottles of a coveted wine vintage, luxury resonates in moments that make life extraordinary.

In hospitality, luxury means anticipating every guest's individual needs and delivering a deeply personalized experience. It is the indulgence of a designer suite, the joy of a thoughtfully curated moment, or the quiet fulfillment of time well spent. As my research study validated, for some, it is the allure of a cherished getaway, for others, it is the simple pleasure of feeling special, confident, and deserving. True luxury lifts the ordinary into something unforgettable, leaving a lasting impression long after the experience has ended.

Luxury can be very personal, yet in professional terms, your product or service may not be what people typically consider to be luxury. You don't need a luxury product or service to offer luxury experiences that will create lasting relationships with your clients.

One of my wealthiest and most generous friends has top-tier status with the airlines and hotel groups, and a substantial real estate portfolio; he is also a philanthropist. Reflecting many people's *initial* impression of luxury, he recently told me that, for him, "luxury is unnecessary." But when I dug deeper, he said that he values things that save him time, for example, VIP queues at the airport or fast lanes on the freeway. So in our conversation we agreed that time is his luxury; saving time means getting more of something he wants and needs. Time—something once spent, you never get back—may be your client's luxury too.

To save time and leverage another's expertise, people often choose luxury services, for example, realtors, stylists, chauffeurs, financial advisors, dry cleaners, and personal shoppers. As a keynote speaker, I invest in hair and makeup teams to come to my hotel room before keynote presentations, because in less than one hour, two people working on my hair and makeup can get me stage-ready. I use that time to meditate, review my speech, relax, and prepare to serve my client. The hair and makeup professionals make sure that I am camera-ready (and sometimes I need to be camera-ready for twelve-plus hours) and will not require touch-ups. They give me the luxury of time.

The message here is clear that, even if you don't provide services in a typical "luxury space," you likely have offerings that your clients can experience as a luxury—whether they use that language for it or not. The underlying principles and systems of luxury can still be powerful tools for building your client relationships.

Champagne Moments, and More

Another finding of the luxury research study was that five words topped the list to describe luxury and a luxury mindset: high-quality, long-lasting, exclusive, unique, and indulgent. Throughout this book, you will see how bringing these qualities into meaningful touchpoints with your clients will heighten their experience of your brand.

In the next chapter, we will consider in more depth how to adopt a luxury mindset to take your relationships with clients from transactional to transformational. I'll then introduce you to the Experience Elevation Model that describes the five luxury levers and how to use them to enhance every aspect of your clients' experience. Think of this model as your client journey framework, or as a movie script in which you are the hero for your clients.

Part two of this book will guide you through the five luxury levers, from the moment you grab your potential client's attention until they become advocates for you, shouting from the rooftops about the products and services you provide. And you will discover strategies to upskill your team to consistently provide exceptional experiences. When you learn to apply luxury principles to your business through the luxury levers, you will begin to gain the mind share of your existing clients. You will be transforming them into advocates who will help draw more business to you.

To inform our exploration of these principles and systems for *Exceptional Experiences*, I interviewed veterans of the luxury industry. You will hear from many of them throughout this book as they add depth and dimension to our understanding of luxury.

At the end of each chapter, in an homage to Madame Clicquot, you will find a champagne moment. Often, leaders are beset by what we might think of as "champagne problems." According to the definition in the *Neen James Dictionary* (think of it as like the *Merriam-Webster* dictionary, only more fun and luxe), champagne problems are not a big deal when compared with other issues like poverty and world wars. (Modern-day philosopher Taylor Swift has her own definition of champagne problems.) We live in a unique time in history. Even in a challenging business landscape, we as leaders are so fortunate in many ways, and sometimes, we lose perspective.

Your challenge, dear reader, is to convert your champagne problems into champagne moments. These are special moments in time when you celebrate something or someone. A champagne moment is an opportunity to pause, reflect, be present, and enjoy. It could be when something extraordinary happens, big or small—a moment that makes you smile, brings you joy, with your heart full... joy that bubbles up, like a glass of champagne! For those of you who do enjoy champagne, you may know that "muselet" is the fancy French word for the wire cage that holds in the cork. The underside of the muselet on a bottle of Veuve Clicquot features a picture of the widow herself. Isn't that a delightful reminder that champagne moments are all around you, personally and professionally, if you pay attention and commit to noticing them?

My clients and friends will tell you that I absolutely love champagne—and a good system. Champagne because, well, it is a celebration in a glass! Good systems because they make everything repeatable and sometimes more reliable. And repeatable execution leads to repeatable results. I aim to share with you systems to lead at the luxury level and bring luxury into every aspect of your business, and I offer you moments of delight that I hope will please you like the bubbles in a glass of champagne.

By the end of our time together, you will understand how to unlock the secrets of the luxury world, build advocates, increase revenue, and differentiate yourself.

Ready for more?

2

Becoming Exceptional

· · · · ·

When you think like a concierge and consistently use luxury, you forge deeper, longer-lasting relationships with your clients. You create the potential for them to become long-term advocates who will champion your brand.

*Luxury is a mindset of excellence,
where thoughtfulness and attention to detail
create meaningful connections.*

Dr. Nido Qubein
president, High Point University

There we were, seated in brand-new plush seats inside the president's suite, eating delicious seafood, when the arena went dark. The light show burst through the darkness, the crowd cheered loudly, and the energy of the stadium was electric. The opening bars of Train's song "Hey, Soul Sister" began to strum, and the audience went crazy! We leapt to our feet, started to dance, and never sat down again throughout the entire night.

Now you might be thinking we were hearing this multi-Grammy and Billboard award winning rock band Train in a big city at a major venue... But no, we were on the campus of High Point University in North Carolina, an education facility that has completely transformed its campus and its community.

Rewind a couple of decades and we would have experienced a starkly different kind of campus.

HPU was historically like many small colleges in the United States, with a transactional approach of the university exchanging a degree for tuition. By the early 2000s, the campus was struggling with declining enrollment. The gardens were unkept. Tired and aging infrastructure drooped about the campus, and perhaps, some might say, the university was a little bland.

That is, until Dr. Nido Qubein changed everything.

When businessman, consultant, author, and undergraduate alumnus Nido Qubein became university president in 2005, HPU went from a run-of-the-mill campus to so much more than an educational facility.

Nido led the transformation of HPU with one focused question: How could he make the university extraordinary? This one word, "extraordinary," drove his decisions and bold choices. To expand the minds of his faculty and students, he created exceptional experiences, exposing them to art and culture, successful thought leaders, and experts in residence including some of the most successful leaders and brands on the planet. Under his leadership, the university hired elite coaches to produce winning sports teams, and he encouraged connection to community, with students completing thousands of hours of service. A case in point: The Train concert performance, in the brand-new Nido and Mariana Qubein Arena and Conference Center as part of the facility's opening weekend, was executed by talented HPU students running the entire show, front and back of house.

HPU prides itself on providing life skills and creating great contributors to society with their practical programs, all in a luxury university setting. Nido is dedicated to anticipating needs, making students feel valued, and delivering meaningful experiences for students, faculty, and visitors. Ensuring that every aspect of HPU reflects the best practices of world-class brands, HPU has drawn on the innovation of Disney, the excellence of The Ritz-Carlton (the university's standards of service are modeled after those of The Ritz), the creativity of Starbucks, and the luxury of Emirates airline.

HPU developed a strong brand reputation as an institution where students gain an education that empowers them to make an impact. HPU alumni become lifelong advocates, contributing to the university's legacy by returning as guest speakers, becoming donors, and encouraging future generations to apply. Nido's philosophy has shifted HPU from a transactional institution to one that offers a truly transformational experience.

The best luxury leaders understand that deepening relationships with new and existing clients can foster a shift from a transactional mindset (where leaders are focused on delivering products or services in exchange for payment), to a transformational mindset (where they are centered on enhancing their clients' life, providing memorable experiences, and building trust).

Think Like a Concierge

One system of elevation that you can apply immediately to shift from transactional to transformational is to think like a concierge.

The word "concierge" originates from the French term "keeper of the keys," the highest level of which is called the Golden Keys/*Les Clefs d'Or*. You might have noticed these elite professionals by their lapel pin featuring two keys. In luxury hotels, the concierge is the most informed, helpful, and connected member of the staff. With the inside scoop on delicious restaurants, private events, and exclusive access, they can help with every request. The concierge, one of the most revered positions in a hotel, is always approachable, friendly, and knowledgeable. They see luxury as a way to build meaningful stories that the hotel and its guests can share for years to come. A concierge mindset transforms routine interactions into memorable moments, elevating every touchpoint from a simple transaction to an opportunity for connection and delight.

The bellhop is another vital role in a hotel and often the source of your first impression. At a luxury hotel, you expect the service of a bellhop to be efficient—they are certainly part of the high-quality experience. They are responsible for guests' luggage (and other services) and are always polite and welcoming. The bellhop's goal is to work quickly and efficiently to move people through the hotel entrance to get them where they need to be.

Too often, leaders act like bellhops, searching for the quickest, most efficient way to move people through the queue, run to the next meeting, get emails out of their inbox, or move on to the next thing on their list. While a manager needs to know how to get things done, a leader needs to know how to lead with luxury and to think like a concierge, exploring opportunities to deepen relationships with clients and teams and considering how to deliver an exceptional experience. You need the vision to make recommendations your clients did not even know they needed.

Matthew Upchurch, CEO of Virtuoso, believes luxury is about delivering beyond expectations through authentic relationships. He cleverly differentiates the company's "luxury travel advisors" from the "travel agents" of its competitors. Virtuoso believes travel advisors fill a vital role on a person's life team. Just like you need a financial advisor, you need a travel advisor to handle the precious commodity of your leisure time. Matthew noted that many luxury travelers desire 24/7 concierges who will maintain a relationship with them across their journeys. When making travel arrangements, they want the benefit of large, well-connected networks as well as personal advisors who respond quickly, know their names, and understand how they like to travel. Consider the difference between booking online through a website (transactional), and partnering with a travel advisor who can help you create memories that will last a lifetime (transformational).

Imagine if, as a leader, if you applied the mindset of a concierge. How would you improve your offerings to create exceptional experiences your team is proud to share with your clients? To move from transactional to transformational, you will need to engage your considerable skills, knowledge, habits, and even your senses, and then leverage them to provide exemplary experiences for your clients.

Top-Tier Clients

In this book, I sometimes refer to top-tier clients. Often of the luxury lover mindset we uncovered in our research study, top-tier clients are ultimately the most influential and valuable brand advocates—loyal customers who genuinely love your brand and voluntarily promote it by sharing positive experiences with friends, family, colleagues, and social media followers. Think of top-tier clients as those who consistently bring significant value to your business, not only through revenue but also through their loyalty, engagement, and positive influence on your brand's reputation. These highly influential advocates contribute to your business's long-term success.

The characteristics of a top-tier client include loyalty, as they consistently choose your business over your competition, and that demonstrates a long-term commitment. They actively engage with your brand with feedback, referrals, and repeat purchases. They resonate with your mission and values. They act like informal ambassadors or brand champions. Through their purchases and by encouraging others to do business with you, they might, over time, contribute significant value.

Top-tier clients have a relationship with you based on trust and mutual respect. They are willing to invest in your business and pay appropriately. They want you both to win, and they believe in supporting you long term.

Over time, your business's top-tier clients and advocates consistently invest their time, attention, and energy, amplifying your brand's reach and cultivating a community of loyal followers who can drive organic growth. Their advocacy enhances your brand's reputation, positioning it as reliable, trustworthy, and customer-focused. By nurturing these relationships, brands create a lasting impact, foster loyalty, and enjoy sustained growth through positive word-of-mouth marketing. Let's help you build deeper relationships with these brand advocates.

The Personal Touch

Every luxury leader I interviewed for this book pointed out that personalization plays a pivotal role in the luxury experience. Do your clients feel a sense of belonging to your brand? Do they realize that you cater to them?

Cornelia Samara, general manager and regional vice president of Four Seasons Hotel Philadelphia, demonstrates that luxury is the art of delivering an unparalleled and deeply personalized experience, responding to the unique desires of each guest. At the Philadelphia hotel, she and her team offer guests a sense of exclusivity and personal service. Her influence is not just local, however. When my husband, Andy, and I were checking into the Four Seasons Sydney, Cornelia organized the general manager there to greet us when we arrived, a lovely personal touch that surprised Andy and delighted me.

When I moved to the United States, the first time I dined at the Four Seasons Philadelphia with Eric Allen,

Think like a concierge, not a bellhop.

· · · · ·

who was the assistant director of catering, the staff handed me a menu printed with my name on it, in pink (anyone who knows me knows pink is my signature color), and my logo! It only cost Eric time and color printing, but that personalization still makes me smile.

Consider how you could personalize your interactions with key clients. Perhaps make a list of the top-tier clients you want to stay connected with this year and mark in your calendar when to update them on changes or exciting news in your company. You could send a customized note that reminds them they are valuable, so they feel they belong. Next time you are reviewing your data analytics report, ask yourself how you could leverage its information to anticipate client needs and preferences and record them in your system for future communications.

Luxury brands understand their clients' preferences in exquisite detail, and they empower their teams to deliver. Leaders can instill a sense of pride and purpose in every team member; they are catalysts for a culture of excellence.

The Importance of Environment

Friends will tell you that when they are guests in my home, I want them to feel like they are in a luxury hotel. I apply my observations from staying in my clients' gorgeous properties to create an experience that is memorable, attentive, and gratifying. My guests receive custom gift boxes stocked with beauty and styling products and warm-weather necessities, always including a Wallaroo hat (because it is a woman-owned company inspired by Australia, whose hats are SPF rated and packable). I live in Tampa, Florida, so the sun is hot. And I believe everyone looks cute in a hat! Our guest room is filled with cozy white robes, reusable slippers, soft bamboo linens, silk pillowcases and sleep masks, earplugs, international travel adapters, a clothes steamer, pj's, a Wi-Fi code, and every travel-sized product you could want. I have equipped it with anything they may have forgotten—and things they didn't even know they needed.

Hosting is my way of showing my guests that I care deeply about them, notice what they enjoy, and tailor the environment to make their stay a memorable, relaxing experience. To do that, I have systems in place: a sense of curiosity for each guest before they arrive, noting their favorite treats, how they take their morning beverage, and food allergies or dislikes. This is all recorded in Evernote and kept for future visits.

Now, imagine how your team would feel if you provided a similar luxury experience for them when they came to your workplace. What little luxury touches could be added to common areas like cafeterias or break rooms, such as building a library of professional development books and magazines to borrow and share, live plants, complimentary beverages and snacks, breakfast items including foods that cater to gluten-free or keto diets? What extra lighting or greenery might you add to staff parking areas or employee entrances to make your people feel welcome and safe? What fun items can you add to the staff notice board to encourage conversation and make people smile? Often, staff areas are overlooked because they are not client-facing. But your team is one of your best investments, because team members are responsible for elevating the client experience. If you make your team feel special and highly valued, they will share that energy with your clients.

Comcast, headquartered in Philadelphia, does a phenomenal job of designing employee-benefit events in their custom theater, the Ralph J. Roberts Forum (affectionately called Town Hall). Comcast's executive director of local media development, Ebonne Ruffins, focuses on learning, with her department hosting thought leaders, training, and special events, as well as celebrating holidays and other meaningful occasions for its teams. The company attends to more than just the physical environment. It regularly conducts employee engagement surveys and leaders often do listening tours. As a result, Comcast is one of the city's largest employers with the most satisfied employees.

The importance of environment extends to client-facing spaces as well. You want clients to feel cared for and confident in you when they visit (or even when they see your background on a video call).

Is it time to replace those out-of-date magazines in your lobby with the latest edition? Or better yet, could you replace them with an elegant coffee-table book? Could you replace that tired, dusty, ugly self-service coffee machine and offer to make visitors fresh coffee instead? Better yet, do you know your client's favorite beverage and could you have it waiting for them when they arrive? Could you stock a mini-fridge with cold brew, sparkling water, and still water to provide choices? Could you replace that fake, dusty greenery with real, living plants? Does your restroom feel mediocre? Could you update it with brighter lighting, luxury scents, artwork, and additional complimentary items, such as hand cream, mouthwash, hair ties, and feminine products? I promise women, especially, notice these details!

Listen with Your Eyes

If you are aware of my work in focus, productivity, and attention, you know my mission in life is for people to feel seen and heard. You may also know that the most famous story in my book *Attention Pays*, and the most requested signature story in my keynotes, is the lesson in attention I received from my then-five-year-old friend Donovan. He reminded me (after a heated debate... have you ever debated with a five-year-old?) that I needed to "listen with my eyes."

Don't just listen with your ears. Listen with your eyes, your heart, and your soul.

As leaders of brands, we sometimes do too much talking and not enough listening. I get it. If you are responsible for revenue, you are constantly exploring how the team can maximize revenue, grow the business, attract new clients. That's what makes you so good at your job!

Listening with your eyes suggests that, as a leader, you are also paying attention to what is not being said. You can read between the lines and hear things that might lead you to more targeted solutions for your clients. This requires you to be 100 percent committed to the conversation, not 100 percent distracted by devices, to-do lists, and running between meetings. It requires you to give your individual attention. That is how luxury hotels provide such memorable, customized experiences—they listen deeply to the conversations of clients and use what they learn to explore delightful ways to surprise them and customize the guest experience.

When someone feels truly, deeply heard by you, it makes an impression on them. If they know you are not distracted but that you are being attentive to their wants and needs, they will trust you more deeply. Your undivided attention is one of the greatest gifts you can give someone. Remember, attention is all about connection. Luxury is about human connection.

Transactional client relationships might be limiting your prospects and affecting revenue. They might be stopping you from creating true advocates for your business or, if your existing clients feel disconnected from your brand, limiting their desire to purchase additional products and services from you. When people feel like they are just a number to an organization, they don't feel any sense of loyalty. Quite the opposite; they may feel a little resentful or, worse, indifferent. Delivering a memorable experience for your clients, with a transformational luxury mindset, will drive loyalty, because it keeps you top of mind. Looking for ways to uplift your clients' lives, and exploring opportunities and systems and processes to make them feel valued, seen, and rewarded, creates deeper, more meaningful relationships with them.

Now that we understand how luxury principles can elevate every interaction in your client's journey, let's explore the Experience Elevation Model—your road map for transforming ordinary touchpoints into extraordinary moments that leave lasting impressions.

CHAMPAGNE MOMENT

What is something that will delight *you*? Is it eating a piece of high-quality, decadent chocolate and feeling it melt in your mouth? Opening the window to feel the cool breeze on your skin? Taking a moment to appreciate a good view? Luxury can be found in these champagne moments, and I am going to encourage you to find more of these moments for yourself (and for your clients, of course).

3

The Experience Elevation Model

· · · · ·

To integrate luxury into your daily operations, systemize it. How? The Experience Elevation Model. It shows how the levers of *entice*, *invite*, *excite*, *delight*, and *ignite* combine to elevate every aspect of your client experience.

*Luxury is a blend of authenticity,
exceptional craftsmanship,
respect for time and nature, and longevity,
resulting in exceptional quality.*

Mathieu Roland-Billecart
CEO, Champagne Billecart-Salmon

Are you a fan of rosé champagne? If so, you can again thank Madame Clicquot for it. Seriously. Not only did she invent the champagne riddling process, but she also developed rosé champagne, or *rosé d'assemblage*. Wanting to create something unique and a magical experience with her champagne, she decided to blend the red grapes from Bouzy (pronounced "boozy"!), France, with the white wine grapes from her vineyard. Voilà—she created rosé champagne.

People already enjoyed her champagne, yet she challenged herself and her team to make their products better. She was obsessed with innovation. Her commitment to excellence reminds us not to get too comfortable, to explore how to step up our offerings so that we attract new clients and retain those that already know us.

In the busyness of daily work, it is easy to be distracted by a growing inbox with emails to answer, another Zoom call to attend, a fire to put out, a proposal to finish, or a networking event to attend. Your growing to-do list might leave you little time to think innovatively or to question how you could make things better for your clients. Systems help address this, because they create freedom. The more systems you have for making everyday decisions, the more valuable real estate you free up in your beautiful brain to focus on the important creative thinking.

Your business's systems might include marketing, customer, and sales funnels or pipelines. These systems are likely repeatable, reliable, and relational (at least to some extent). Luxury asks you to elevate every aspect of your business, so that you consistently deliver exceptional experiences to your clients. The Experience Elevation Model, which includes the five luxury levers that we will explore in detail in part two, offers a system to incorporate luxury principles into your business.

Experience Elevation Model™

Market share

Create advocates	**Ignite**	Who else can I tell about my experience?
Offer exclusivity	**Delight**	How did they anticipate needs I didn't even know I had?
Elevate experience	**Excite**	What else will they do?
Demonstrate experience	**Invite**	How do I get access to that special level?
Capture attention	**Entice**	Why should I pay attention to you?

Mind share

This model enhances the typical client journey, engaging the knowledge uncovered in the luxury mindset research and two fundamental principles of delivering luxury experiences: anticipating needs and providing clients with exclusive access. You will also discover that once a client is exposed to your brand's top-of-the-line offering and exceptional service, they will be unsatisfied with a lesser experience.

The Experience Elevation Model builds on the well-known AIDA marketing model, created by Elias St. Elmo Lewis. The acronym AIDA stands for attention, interest, desire, and action. It is an advertising effect model based on behavioral psychology that identifies six stages a consumer goes through to decide about purchasing a product or service. It draws from the hierarchy of effects, which explains how advertising influences a consumer's decision to buy a product or service, from awareness to knowledge, liking, preference, conviction, and finally purchase. The model suggests that brands guide consumers through all six stages, which can be divided into three main categories: cognitive, affective, and behavioral—or think, feel, and do.

The Experience Elevation Model is a refinement of AIDA. It consists of five luxury levers meant to engage luxury principles and characteristics. The model illustrates what will prompt your clients and prospective clients to think of you, to take action to work with you, and then to tell others about what you do—just like that. Each luxury lever in the Experience Elevation Model prompts you to answer key questions your clients are asking about you, whether to you directly or to themselves and their close advisors.

At the first level of *entice*, where you can elevate your business in the eyes of your potential customers, you need to answer their question, "Why should I pay attention to you?" Once you have earned their attention, you need to show them that you see them, while you also motivate them to earn entry into your product or service. At the level of *invite*, you are answering the question, "How do I get access to that special level?" to deepen their engagement with you. Then you engage the lever *excite* to build their anticipation and show them they are worth the investment in your product or service, answering the question, "What else will they do?" This is where you delight your clients by exceeding their expectations and deepening their connection to you and your brand even further. You leave them asking themselves, "How did they anticipate needs I didn't even know I had?" From this place of *delight*, you engage the lever *ignite*, building long-term advocates who become like an extension of your sales team and brand. Your clients are asking, "Who else can I tell about my experience?"

Whether you are a solopreneur as a team of one or a Fortune 500 company with thousands of people, you can incorporate each luxury lever in the Experience Elevation Model into your systems. In the coming chapters, we will explore this process in depth. But before we move on to the first lever, let's look at Delta Air Lines as an example of how the Experience Elevation Model can work.

Elevate expectations: turn the excellent into the exceptional.

......

Luxury Lever 1: Entice

To entice clients and captivate them requires offering unique, personalized, and exclusive experiences, making them feel special and valued from the first interaction.

Tim Mapes, SVP and chief communications officer at Delta Air Lines, believes in differentiating the company's strategy by providing unique services that make every customer feel special.

Delta focuses on attracting luxury travelers by paying attention to details, understanding that once a passenger has experienced certain perks of premium flying, they rarely want to go back to economy. The company has created swanky Delta One Lounges, has a sommelier assist with wine choices, and has engaged luxury designer Missoni for exquisite custom amenities and design elements in both the Delta One Lounge and onboard; in select cities, Delta even offers first-class passengers popular Shake Shack burgers. By focusing on quality, comfort, and ease for passengers, the airline stands out among its competitors.

As a Delta passenger myself, I felt very spoiled to enjoy the Delta One experience of flying home to Australia to see my mum for the holidays. Before the trip even began, Delta communicated what the experience would be like, letting me know that as a Delta One international flyer, I would have complimentary access to the Delta One Lounge; spacious, fully adjustable, lie-flat beds and cozy bedding mattress pads on flight; delicious meals; and comfort and safety for the long-haul trip. They mention all of this on their website, in advertising, and in personalized email messaging I received before the trip, but reading about it and experiencing it first-hand were totally different.

Arriving at the LA airport, I adored Delta's dedicated check-in area, complimentary beverages, and private security screening at the Delta One Lounge, allowing me to check my bags quickly and efficiently. The moment the glass doors to the lounge opened, I instantly felt like I had entered a retreat, a peaceful sanctuary where the team was genuinely excited to see me. It was like checking in to a spa. I loved the dedicated restaurant, sushi bar, shower suites, artwork, wellness lounge (including napping pods and recovery tools like a Hyperice massager and compression boots for tired legs).

Luxury Lever 2: Invite

The luxury lever *invite* is about demonstrating your experience and creating a sense of belonging, where clients feel like they want to be part of an exclusive, maybe even elite, circle. This draws clients further into your brand experience.

Delta uses data-driven systems to personalize clients' travel experiences, regardless of whether they are flying coach or first class. For example, by knowing a frequent flyer's preferences through their SkyMiles profile, the company can cater to the passenger's seating preference or favorite in-flight amenities. Delta can tailor a seamless journey from the moment a customer books their flight, promising them comfort in all interactions.

The details embedded in Delta's systems foster a sense of loyalty and belonging that clients want to maintain. For example, you see your name on the in-seat screen when logged in to in-flight entertainment. This system remembers the movies you are watching, so (if you are like me) you might start watching a movie on one flight and then, on an entirely different flight, resume it where you left off—fabulous personalization!

Luxury Lever 3: Excite

Excitement is creating memorable, share-worthy, surprising experiences that encourage clients to engage with your brand. This requires you to lead with curiosity and engage your team in ways to heighten the client journey.

Delta masters the art of anticipating and delighting travelers through carefully orchestrated moments that engage all of the senses. As a SkyMiles member, you might receive an unexpected text about a complimentary upgrade to first class, or arrive at your gate to find your family thoughtfully seated together—even on that last-minute booking you were worried about. These aren't random acts of kindness, but rather part of Delta's systematic approach to creating memorable experiences.

Even in moments of stress, Delta's customer service transforms potential frustrations into demonstrations of care. Their phone representatives don't just solve problems—they own them. During my research, I discovered countless stories of agents who went beyond standard solutions, whether rerouting passengers around weather delays or ensuring a traveler made it to an important family event. What stood out wasn't just their efficiency, but their genuine enthusiasm for turning travel challenges into opportunities to showcase exceptional service.

Luxury Lever 4: Delight

To delight clients, you must go beyond the ordinary, beyond expectations, with thoughtful, personalized touches that leave a lasting positive impact.

One of the most compelling (and most often shared on social media) stories is offered to select Diamond Medallion level members with tight connections at certain airport hubs: Delta's complimentary airport transfer service via a Porsche. This service is not guaranteed and cannot be requested or purchased directly, although the lucky passenger is told in advance. They receive a planeside transfer to a connecting flight in a Porsche. The Porsche transfer makes premium clients feel valued, like they are part of an elite group. They may not have known they needed this wonderful perk, but once they have experienced it, they want it all the time!

Luxury Lever 5: Ignite

Igniting passion among clients is about turning them into advocates for your brand.

Delta ultimately ignites loyalty because its employee-first culture empowers staff. The airline makes employees feel valued, and the employees extend this feeling to the company's customers, who receive consistently exceptional service. This turns customers into loyal advocates who actively promote the airline to their networks through personal recommendations and social media sharing.

Delta Diamond Medallion members are a perfect example. Often fierce advocates for the brand, they share about flights on social media shout-outs and sometimes even opt for connecting flights over a direct route, just so they can travel with Delta. And remember that many people consider time a luxury! They willingly spend their time and money, because they love flying with Delta.

Delta does not consider itself to be in the business of just selling flights; its leadership and employees believe they are creating lifelong relationships with their customers, who become vocal advocates for the brand because it provides luxury experiences that create memories.

We are about to move on to part two, where we will explore each of these levers in more detail, including the systems you can implement to apply lessons from luxury to the client journey with your business. There are different types of systems designed to be integrated into almost any setting.

Throughout this book, I encourage you to take on the challenge of a more systemized approach. Take stock of what systems you already have in place so that, as we move into part two and begin our exploration of the first lever, *entice*, you can explore how to leverage luxury to elevate all your systems.

CHAMPAGNE MOMENT

How might you elevate a system that you use or something that you do daily? Perhaps play your favorite music during your morning coffee? Go out for a nice lunch instead of eating at your desk? Include time in the sauna with your trip to the gym? Choose one thing to enhance the level of a regular activity and enjoy it.

PART TWO

Five Luxury Levers

4

Captivating Experience

· · · · ·

The luxury lever *entice* involves paying close attention to your clients, creating an emotional connection, and doing so through engaging storytelling. To entice means to appeal to clients in a new way, when they are asking, "Why should I pay attention to you?"

Luxury transforms routine interactions into memorable moments that clients want to share.

Philippe Hertzberg
founder, Secret Journeys

Madame Clicquot wanted people worldwide to experience her champagne. In the early years of the 1800s, during the Napoleonic Wars, she smuggled thousands of bottles by boat, in coffee barrels, so that when the wars were over, her champagne would be used for celebrations. She interested Napoleon and the Russian czar with her champagne, creating a wider desire for her product, because it was associated with elite people.

As a leader, you may be responsible for increasing market share of your business or the mind share of your clients. Often leaders overinvest time, attention, and resources in trying to gain new clients, and then once they become clients, assume they will stay. But that is not the reality in business today. Luxury leaders can teach us that we need not only to appeal to new clients, but must also invest attention in existing clients. The lever *entice* is about creatively getting a client's attention to connect with them emotionally.

Trying to attract clients the same way your competitors do will not help you stand out. Typically, brands rely on loyalty, quality products, multigenerational recommendations, category dominance, or brand identity to differentiate themselves and retain clients. Those areas are important, and maybe they used to be enough, but in today's competitive landscape for client attention, they're no longer sufficient. Often, brands overestimate their client loyalty and underestimate the impact of paying personalized attention.

Pay Attention

If you've ever heard people say that our attention span is declining, that's rubbish! Our attention span is not declining. Our attention is *split*. There are so many distractions pulling us in all directions at any given time. Brands are in a war for our most coveted resource: attention. According to a 2021 article in *Forbes*, over 23 billion text messages are sent worldwide daily, and the number will only keep growing; most people are exposed to between 150 and 500-plus messages a day, and the numbers are even higher for executives. The combination of email, print, television, social media, billboards, text messages, Zoom calls, Teams messages, instant messages, Slack messages, video messages, voice notes, and phone calls leaves everyone exhausted and distracted.

To make clients feel special and valued, you must earn their attention through emotional connections, consistently delivering personalized attention and service that caters to their unique preferences and needs.

Hospitals may not be the first thing that comes to mind when you think about luxury experiences, but I have worked with several hospitals to help them adopt concierge-level, patient-centered approaches to meet medical needs, promote comfort and convenience, and reduce stress for patients and their families. To attract new clients (patients), they implemented systems such as introducing dedicated reception areas for VIPs, sharing physicians' private contact numbers with patients, and upskilling vital staff in customer-service training and hospitality programs. They paid special attention to creating a well-designed environment that feels and looks luxurious, with calming colors, private nursing, premium suites, translation services, state-of-the-art equipment, travel planning, accommodations, and chef-prepared, high-quality meals. In challenging and high-stress environments, this attention to detail fosters loyalty and satisfaction, which are critical to a hospital's reputation and long-term patient retention.

Consider this: What services could you offer that will improve client satisfaction and allow your staff to focus more on direct client care, regardless of the offerings you provide?

Share Your Story

One way to create an emotional connection with your clients that will draw their attention is to share your story. To feel more aligned with you, your clients want to feel like they know you. They want to know why you make decisions, your backstory, your history, what influences your offerings. And they look for the consistency between your values and beliefs and theirs. People learn through stories. In his TED Talk "The Clues to a Great Story," Andrew Stanton, writer and director of Pixar's *Toy Story* and *WALL-E*, says, "We are born problem solvers; stories deepen our understanding as human beings." Stories help us connect to a brand, identify with experiences and characters, engage our imaginations, and change how we see the world. Think of stories as the glue that makes ideas stick.

Investing in upskilling your team to become great (or even better) storytellers will pay off in terms of client engagement, online and offline. Undoubtedly, your business has some great stories. Hospitals are filled with heartwarming, life-saving examples; media does impactful work in the community in education and diversity; luxury travel with a focus on sustainability provides small villages with life-giving work... These are examples from some of my clients. *You, too*, can mine your work for great stories to tell about your brand, and I bet your clients want to hear them!

Create characters, give them depth, and let clients see themselves in your examples. Take care when telling a story; make it personal and relatable to those hearing it in the room or reading it on their own. As a storyteller, make your audience (client) a promise that your story is worth their attention. Even better, create what my friend and keynote director Mike Ganino calls a retellable story.

Paris-based Philippe Hertzberg, founder of private-access luxury tour company Secret Journeys, shares his love and respect for Paris with guests visiting his amazing city. His company became so popular that he expanded into New York City, and every person fortunate enough to spend time with him raves about the unique adventures he curates. Having had a previous career immersed in narrative journalism at *The New York Times*, *International Herald Tribune*, and Lonely Planet, he believes in the power of storytelling to engage and inspire curiosity while preserving a city's heritage.

When speaking of his beloved City of Lights, he said, "Paris is a place, a promise, a mystery, a dream. Whether you are visiting for the first time or the hundredth, there is always something new to discover. Our deep knowledge and personal connections, combined with the art of storytelling, will open doors to a Paris that you never imagined—and will never forget." Memories are anchored in emotions, and storytelling promotes emotional connection. Secret Journeys' tour guides are called storytellers, and they collaborate with destinations to bring each guest's tour to life

Brands overestimate
client loyalty
and underestimate
personalized
attention.

.....

in unique ways—whether that is through a private-access tour of the hydraulic elevator of the Eiffel Tower (topped with a glass of champagne and a limited-edition macaroon tasting by the world-renowned pastry chef Pierre Hermé) or a private backstage tour with a special performance at the Palais Garnier opera house. His storytellers pay attention to every detail to create high-quality experiences and long-lasting memories.

Here is a tip I heard from Erin King, creator of the Energy Exam and cofounder of the Energy Institute, about three great phrases to bring energy to the beginning of your story:

- So there you are...
- Imagine you...
- Have you ever...

You can use these prompts as a storytelling system to engage your audience.

Share Your Heritage

Your brand's heritage is more than just background information; how you tell your origin story and the history of your company can build emotional connections with clients. Investing in your product creates an association between the client and your company's history. Consider which elements of your brand's heritage would appeal to your ideal client. What narrative about your products' evolution, craftsmanship, or legacy could convey that they are more than just items for sale? What story would entice clients to invest in your service's prestige?

The fashion house Chanel's heritage is woven into the very atmosphere of its stores. Walk into any Chanel boutique, and you are immersed in the brand's rich history, as sales associates expertly and affectionately recount the iconic tales of Gabrielle Bonheur Chanel (a.k.a. Coco) and her innovative designs. The names of products, the packaging, the merchandising—every detail is intentional and rooted in the brand's legendary past. Take the 31 Le Rouge refillable lipstick collection. The lipstick is presented in a sleek mirrored box that pays homage to the iconic mirrored staircase in Chanel's apartment on rue Cambon, where she would observe her models before each show. Clients who know about this connection to Chanel's creative world come to feel that their lipstick is more than a simple beauty item. It is a piece connected to a rich history. Every time they apply their lipstick, clients feel connected to the brand's legacy—and to Coco herself. Of course, Chanel associates share these stories, making the connections for clients and ensuring they feel a part of something greater: a tradition of timeless elegance.

Collaborate Creatively

Creative collaborations can help you leverage another business's strengths while that business leverages yours, to elevate both your offerings. Strategic collaborations can help you expand your clientele, capture new markets, and offer fresh, engaging experiences that strengthen your brand's reputation. How can you reimagine what is possible in your industry to create unforgettable, meaningful moments for clients? Who do you want to forge relationships with to make your brand even more enticing to your clients?

While giving a keynote for the executive team at Fairmont Hotels in Canada, I had the privilege to stay at the Fairmont Tremblant in the Laurentian mountains. Only one challenge for this little Floridian... It was the middle of winter! Knowing I would not have the right gear for the frigid weather, one of the hotel's team members greeted me with a most glorious Canada Goose jacket. Wearing that jacket felt like a constant cuddle! The hotel has a special partnership where Canada Goose loans them jackets to share with their guests. Genius! This simple, impactful collaboration provides an exceptional experience. Secretly I wanted to keep the coat! I loved it! Being part of that exceptional experience, I now have a deeper awareness of Canada Goose, and each time I see the brand I am reminded of my fairy-tale stay at the Fairmont Tremblant. I imagine that is why hotels use wonderfully branded amenities; each time their guest enjoys that brand in the future, they are reminded of their stay.

There are myriad examples of ways you could collaborate to raise the experience for your clients. In a lovely celebration of shared craftsmanship and heritage, champagne maison Billecart-Salmon partnered with bespoke tailor Huntsman Savile Row to create an exclusive tweed fabric. Who knew we needed this collaboration? But it embodies the good taste and elegance of both businesses. Mathieu Roland-Billecart, the seventh-generation CEO, believes in partnering with like-minded brands committed to superior luxury experiences. The tweed, inspired by the champagne's terroir (a French term for the environmental factors that affect the grapes) and the artistry of Billecart-Salmon, features a silver-gray base reminiscent of the stainless steel tanks and silver foil used in champagne production, with accents of green to represent the vines, purple to highlight the pinot noir grapes, and soft white representing flowers of the vines and the foam when champagne is poured in a glass. It is lovely to hear where inspiration comes from.

Creative partnerships like these can captivate attention in a crowded market. They benefit both parties when they offer a unique product or service that marries the strengths of each brand. Seek out innovative collaborations that will attract new clients for both partners and add value for existing advocates of both brands. This will enhance brand visibility and desirability for both businesses. What might happen when you think outside your industry or the accepted way of doing something? How might you be inspired by, and leverage, other brands or industries that appeal to similar clients?

Of the Billecart-Salmon partnership with Huntsman Savile Row, Mathieu shared, "We are strong believers in value-based partnerships. The Huntsman team are friends of ours who share the same passion for exceptional quality and respect for centuries-long heritage. We already had many clients in common. In a world dominated by big corporations, it is nice when small independents can get together to showcase what we do to a wider audience."

When you lead a strategy that focuses on paying attention and sharing your story, you are laying the foundations to entice your clients. Highlighting your heritage and showcasing your thinking helps people understand and connect with your brand. If you combine these strategies with finding creative ways to collaborate, you are destined to attract potential new clients to your brand and remind existing clients why they enjoy working with you. That not only helps you stay top of mind, but it differentiates your brand from your competitors. These strategies set the scene to allow you to communicate even more powerfully with them and invite them to do business with you.

CHAMPAGNE MOMENT

Stories surround us in the most delightful ways. Tonight, could you immerse yourself in storytelling that fills your soul? Perhaps it's sinking into a plush theater seat as the curtain rises, or gathering friends for the big game with delicious snacks and perfectly chilled champagne (or sparkling water, of course). Choose an experience that makes your heart dance—one that will become its own story worth sharing. Create this moment with intention, knowing that the best stories aren't just told—they're felt, lived, and savored.

5

Demonstrating Experience

· · · · ·

You can transform how you communicate, making your offerings feel exclusive, sophisticated, and desirable. The luxury lever *invite* is about more than just words. It is about your overall communication strategy. Exceptional communication intrigues and inspires your clients to ask, "How do I get access to that special level?"

Luxury is all the little things—attention to detail that goes beyond the usual, an insight that becomes an unexpected but welcomed feature, or a piece of data that creates an extraordinary connection or experience.

Michael Barber
chief marketing officer, StarTech.com

As a little girl, I was often the "new kid" at school. You never forget that awkward feeling: all eyes on you, dressed in a second-hand uniform or hand-me-down clothes, as the whole room assesses you from head to toe to see if you "fit in" to their circle or standards. Those first impressions determine if you will be invited to be part of the cool kids, sporty kids, nerdy smarty-pants kids, or tough kids.

Being the outsider meant understanding the need for belonging, acceptance, popularity, and wanting to be liked (when we get older, we realize how crazy that is). When new students joined a school I was already attending, I was the self-appointed welcome committee (knowing that "new kid" feeling), ensuring they knew how to navigate the building, had someone to sit with at lunch, and had the inside scoop on which teachers were mean and who was cool. I wanted them to feel invited, engaged, and safe.

With so much practice entering new spaces alone, I developed skills to assess people's intentions, to step into school leadership roles and instantly take charge. This skill, developed at a young age, serves me well as an executive coach with senior leaders, where I must quickly assess people's comfort levels and obstacles so they openly share about challenges we can solve together with specific, customized strategies.

You can make someone feel welcome and safe, and let them know they belong, with strong, confident communication. But before you can decide on the language you are going to use, you need clarity on the type of clients you want to invite into your organization.

Building a client profile could include important characteristics like demographics, psychographics, behaviors and habits, emotional and social drivers, brand fit, and lifestyle choices. Sometimes marketers call them avatars or personas. This knowledge helps you create compelling invitations that resonate deeply with your ideal clients, fostering trust and encouraging long-term relationships. It is also important to know which of the luxury mindsets you want to attract, because that will influence your language, visuals, events and experiences, and how you direct your client attraction strategy.

Recall that the four main luxury mindsets are reluctant and removed (finds luxury hard); the pro prioritizer (uses luxury for their career and reputation); the confident and content (does not prioritize luxury); and the luxury lover (believes everyone deserves luxury every day). Each mindset values luxury differently and speaks a different luxury language.

The reluctant and removed mindset thinks luxury is hard. Someone with this mindset does not think brands understand them. They feel busy and overwhelmed. While you may not want to focus marketing efforts on attracting this mindset, you must realize that you already have them as clients, and when this mindset is making decisions to buy from you, it's important to be able to speak their luxury language. Share how you or your product will:

- help them relax and reward themselves
- make their lives easier and/or more efficient
- reduce overwhelm or busyness
- remove/reduce hassle, frustration, and worry

People with the pro prioritizer mindset think luxury is power and use it to further their careers and reputations. Our research showed that they are also potential brand champions if your brand is aligned with their values and has proven longevity and reliability. They will share your brand with people they are mentoring or work with, and they value professional development. When communicating with this mindset, share how you or your product:

- helps them feel more confident
- will be perceived as high-quality, sophisticated, and authentic
- is socially conscious and environmentally sustainable
- is a reward for hard work and accomplishment in their career

- influences personal growth and development
- improves reputation, appearance, and the impression they make

People with the confident and content mindset think, "I've got this!" and they like to create memories for people they care about. They feel good about their purchasing decisions. They want to know how you and your product will:

- improve connection with their friends and family
- improve their quality of life
- provide more memorable experiences
- give greater satisfaction in their career and life

Those with the luxury lover mindset believe, "I'm worth it." They like to share their love of exclusivity and luxury, and I often say they have "big mouths," meaning they want to share their experiences with the world, making them great potential advocates for you. They want to hear you use words and phrases that demonstrate how you or your product will:

- offer exclusive and unique opportunities, and behind-the-scenes access
- personalize and customize your offerings
- recognize and reward them for a sense of accomplishment
- improve their professional and social status

So, what do you do now with all this knowledge on luxury mindsets and the luxury language they want and need to hear? Review your sales process and marketing collaterals, your sales training and sales scripts, to align your resources with your client attraction strategy. Review your materials for your retention strategy. Assess materials for key words and promises and invitations to align with your attraction strategy. Design marketing advertising specifically for the luxury mindsets you want to attract. You can download an executive summary of the research on the Luxury Mindset website (luxuryisamindset.com).

To appeal to the different types of people you want to attract, you need to be able to communicate your overarching vision—the *why* behind your brand—as well as delivering the *what* with precision and attention to detail. Have you ever noticed an airport café offering ready-made examples of each meal, and yet they still hand you a menu? This ensures people who see what they want (and don't care about the ingredients) will order on sight, and those who want to know all the options, including calorie count or even where items are sourced, will peruse the menu. Neither approach is better; they're just different. But combining them ensures you appeal both to global thinkers (who focus on the big picture) and local thinkers (who focus on details). How might one element of your brand communication (an exclusive offer, a social media campaign, a LinkedIn post) appeal to both audiences?

Roll Out the Red Carpet

When you watch a movie premiere or awards show on television and see celebrities walk the red carpet in their stunning outfits, exquisite jewels, divine shoes, perfect hair and makeup, and big smiles for the cameras, do you ever wonder if they diet for weeks to fit into that gown or tux? No? Just me? Behind the scenes, their crew works for hours so they can confidently and glamorously walk the red carpet. We "roll out the red carpet" for celebrities at movie premieres. How much fun would it be to roll out the red carpet for our clients? To do this, you need to understand what makes them feel special.

In our luxury mindset research, we found that making clients feel seen and appreciated—a.k.a. personalization—increases their likelihood of making a purchase. We also discovered that leaders are more likely to make a purchase if they are familiar with the brand, with 56 percent of those surveyed saying previous experience with a brand most influences their purchasing decisions.

We discovered that leaders desire a quality experience, with 72 percent of leaders prioritizing "quality" as the defining trait of luxury. When investigating the influence of unique opportunities, we found that luxury lovers and pro prioritizers are more likely to advocate for brands that make them feel valued. They appreciate exclusive events, or private shopping hours or special access, just like red-carpet experiences. Despite thinking differently about

Personalization requires information. Customization requires connection. Fascination requires anticipation, which is the heart of luxury.

· · · · ·

luxury, all four luxury mindsets agreed that experiences where brands were thoughtful and attentive reinforced the emotional significance of their purchase, and that created a lasting impression. But realistically, how can you personalize for everyone?

Lisa Holland, CEO of Sheltair, the largest privately owned aviation network in the United States, has a family-first culture. Her team is renowned for going above and beyond to ensure clients feel valued and understood. Sheltair's clients are often pressed for time, making it crucial for the company to find meaningful ways to connect and provide seamless, personalized experiences where every detail is crafted to exceed expectations. Lisa says, "When time is a luxury our clients can't afford, we train and empower our team to go the extra mile. We focus on getting to know them personally and understanding their unique needs." Her team members also make small gestures like providing dog treats for clients' pets, remembering pets' names, or knowing their clients' favorite coffee. These personal touches all show genuine care.

When people fly private at a Sheltair FBO (fixed base operator), the linesmen place a red mat (symbolizing the red carpet) for passengers at the steps of the private jet. If it is a company jet, the mat features that company's logo. This simple and fun system gives passengers a literal red-carpet experience that makes them smile as they are disembarking. Everyone feels special, *even though* the organizational practice is the same.

How could you advance experiences for your clients so they look forward to hearing from you, meeting with you, and interacting with your business? These are universal desires. What could you do before they even arrive at your (real or virtual) door to engage them and build anticipation of the experience they will have with you? To stay top of mind with clients, you need to balance a variety of communication modes and regular touchpoints, remembering that people have busy calendars and full lives, juggling personal and professional commitments. Focusing on quality, exclusivity, and emotional connection will help you deliver exceptional, red-carpet-style experiences that linger. Here are some ideas that might inspire you, because they tap into associations with luxury that we saw across all four luxury mindsets.

Offer a personal concierge service: Which high-touch services could you offer to anticipate client needs? Could you have a dedicated team member as the first contact point, so clients feel like they have their own concierge, to create an aura of exclusivity and effortless luxury?

Build bespoke welcome experiences: How might you treat your clients to a custom welcome that mirrors the intimacy and elegance of luxury brands? Louis Vuitton encourages people to make appointments at their retail store; someone greets you at the door, asks you a few questions, and then assigns a sales associate to you.

Provide seamless access: How could every interaction feel like an invitation to a world of exclusivity? Offer your clients privileged access to products, services, or experiences not available to the public—whether it's an early look at a new product, access to a private showroom, or a behind-the-scenes tour. This "members-only" level reinforces that your clients are part of an elite circle.

You could give clients a red-carpet experience and a sneak peek into your business with access to leadership and decision makers, the engineers who design your products, and administrative and operational support, so they have faces to put to the names behind company emails. Perhaps you could have team members create short videos to share.

Now you know about the complimentary Delta/Porsche plane-side service mentioned in chapter 3. What is your brand's version of that? Could you offer a meeting with the chef in a restaurant? With the general manager of the hotel? The owner of the luxury real estate firm? The founder of your company, your longest-serving bellhop or receptionist, the designer or head stylist? What about coffee with the senior researchers or leadership? Who on your team would your clients most love to meet? Let's get your top-tier clients, especially those luxury lovers and pro prioritizers, in front of them!

At your next team meeting, ask your people to brainstorm this concept of red-carpet experiences for clients, and make a list of ideas that can be reviewed to find the gems. Embrace all the ideas and choose one or two you can pilot in the next ninety days. I use the word "pilot" often when coaching and consulting with clients, because that gives you permission to try something new, get feedback, modify it, incorporate it, and re-evaluate the effectiveness before you roll it out. Sharing that it is a pilot project with your top-tier clients shows them that they belong in your trusted circle, turning even your own research into a luxury experience! That can deepen their loyalty to you. If you do include clients, seek their feedback, listen deeply, and then let them know what you incorporated based on their recommendations. When I first wrote *Attention Pays*, I created a two-day workshop and offered it as a pilot course to one of my best clients. I made a lot of changes to the content based on their valuable feedback. Sometimes we are too close to our product design or project scope, and seeking our trusted clients' input can evolve our thinking and the end deliverable.

Luxury Language Builds Lasting Relationships

Every touchpoint with your client communicates something about you. Words, tone, colors, textures, body language, advertisements, emails, voicemails, social media posts, mailouts, posters, digital signage, elevators, parking lots, and meetings all matter.

When was the last time you conducted an audit of all of your messaging? My challenge to you is to gather all your print marketing collateral on one table and investigate if all the elements look and feel like the luxury experience you want clients to have. Is the message consistent? Do you use language that appeals to your top-tier clients? Do they speak the luxury language (more on that below) of the mindsets you want to attract? Make it your mission this week to send your team on a treasure hunt to notice every piece of paper, every sign, every place your logo appears, and then compare notes to look for dated or incorrect materials. The results might surprise you.

Luxury language is an essential tool in your leadership toolkit for building lasting relationships with repeat top-tier clients—those who value exclusivity, high-quality service, and personalized experiences. The luxury mindset research revealed that specific terms such as "bespoke," "exquisite," and "timeless" evoke a sense of sophistication and prestige. Using this language fosters deeper emotional connections and signals that your brand understands and prioritizes your clients' unique needs and aspirations. Luxury language not only elevates your brand perception but also encourages client loyalty and advocacy. By consistently integrating these elements across all touchpoints, you can create exceptional experiences that justify premium pricing, boost revenue, and keep clients returning. Thoughtful, tailored communications transform regular interactions into memorable moments, ensuring top-tier clients feel valued and invested in the brand's ongoing success.

The luxury mindset research showed that all types of mindsets value high-quality products and services, so whichever type of client you are appealing to, highlight quality, exclusivity, and sophistication. Pro prioritizers and luxury lovers, in particular, seek exclusivity and authenticity. Use language in marketing materials that emphasizes craftsmanship, durability, and the unique qualities of your offering. For example:

- "Handcrafted with precision for discerning individuals."
- "Experience the exclusivity of [a product/service] tailored just for you."

Consider offering limited-edition items or experiences and communicate their exclusivity through campaign messages such as "Only 100 available worldwide."

Some people in our study associated purchases with self-worth, indulgence, and achievement. Personalization enhances their feeling of being valued and special. You can customize their buying experience with tailored recommendations and exclusive consultations. Use messaging such as:

- "Because you deserve nothing but the best."
- "Celebrate your achievements with something extraordinary."

Send personalized thank-you notes or post-purchase offers that align with your customers' preferences.

First-Class Communications

Matthew Upchurch, CEO of Virtuoso, shared that his travel advisors often ask their clients, "How do you want to feel on this trip? How do you want to feel when it is over?" I love these questions because they allow travel advisors to design the perfect experience and environment to make that client's wishes come true.

A list of thoughtful, open-ended questions is critical to delivering a customized experience for your clients to feel seen and special. Do not overwhelm them with lengthy forms, but focus on a few impactful questions that get to the heart of their needs and desires. Before keynoting for clients, I conduct many phone interviews with key stakeholders, using specific questions that provide insight into how I need to tailor messages for their audience. These questions are a system designed to capture meaningful insights, enabling me to deliver customized examples that resonate deeply with the audience. It's not uncommon for audience members to say, "Wow, you know our KPIs/challenges/industry so well" or "How long have you worked here?" These are the greatest compliments. This system of questions accelerates my preparation time and allows me to customize my presentation for them.

Asking questions that go beyond the collection of surface-level information allows you to better understand your clients' needs. Imagine a financial advisor meeting a new client. If, instead of starting with the basic questions—"What's your income?" "What are your financial goals?"—they found better ways to connect, they might ask: "What are the biggest challenges you anticipate in the next twelve months?" "What is the best way I can add value to our conversation today?" "Is there anything else I need to be aware of before I make my recommendations?" Questions are not just about gathering information; they are about demonstrating your commitment to creating an exceptional, personalized experience.

Many people experience you first through your digital footprint—your website, email, and social media. Perhaps you grab their attention on social media, so they click on your bio, which takes them to your website, where they download a free digital asset. And then they begin receiving emails from you.

When was the last time you visited your online profiles? When was the last time you reviewed your LinkedIn profile? (Think of LinkedIn like your own personal website.) Not because you are looking for a new job, but because it can be a talent-attraction strategy for your organization. If you haven't done it for a while, pull up your website or online platform and ask yourself if it feels first class. Does it look and feel high-quality? Do you need to change any of the imagery, visuals, or language to be more inclusive or sound more concierge-like, as if your ideal client is reading copy written just for them? If you haven't reviewed your "about us" page, social media bio, email signature, or voicemail message in the past thirty days, let me gently remind you to spend fifteen minutes this week reviewing these digital experiences to ensure they convey the feeling you want people to have of you, and your brand, when they meet you online.

Also pay particular attention to tailoring your digital messages. As world-renowned marketing expert Michael Barber pointed out to me in a high-energy conversation, digital messaging—email, text messages, DMs—in the luxury sector always feel tailored and personal, not just by name but by past behaviors and interests. And a little word of caution here: Some of your most dedicated customers hear from you regularly, and if they sense that your automatic text is not tailored for them, but is the same message everyone else is getting, it feels less special. Make it personal so it feels as though the communication is one-on-one.

In our digital world, you can use analog systems to garner attention. Even the smallest gesture of luxury can make a big difference—this is true of people you serve, and of people who serve you. When I am in the "silly season" of the speaking calendar (that's what our team calls the spring and fall, because of the volume of keynote speeches and flights), I sometimes use the hotel laundry service (I refuse to check a bag, even for long international adventures). While staying at the stunning Mandarin Oriental Ritz in Madrid, I sent my travel clothes for laundry and one of the pieces went missing for a few hours. What surprised me the most was that when it was found, the team sent a handwritten apology signed by the whole housekeeping department, along with a bag of goodies, including shoe trees, Do Not Disturb signs, lint removal items, and many fun housekeeping amenities. Their kindness blew me away! They took a minor problem (a champagne problem) and turned it into a champagne moment, a delightful memory from my stay with them.

Handwritten notes are symbolic of care and attention to detail demonstrating appreciation. They mean the world because the recipient knows the time it took to create them.

Every client touchpoint, whether through technology or personal outreach, needs be crafted to make clients feel valued and intimately connected to your brand. You can enhance client communications through a blend of digital and analog methods. The tables on the following pages outline a few key tactics for each and their benefits. These methodologies position your brand as thoughtful, premium, and client-centric, driving differentiation and revenue growth. While not all of the methods will work for every business, try choosing two from each category that fit into your business's overall branding.

Digital Communication Methods

Personalized email campaigns	Allow you to segment and tailor content, showing your understanding of your clients' needs and leading to higher engagement and trust
Exclusive VIP or invitation-only newsletters	Make valued clients feel privileged and connected to your brand's inner circle
Custom mobile apps	Provide exclusive, personalized access to services, enhancing convenience and brand interaction
Video messages	One of my favorite ways to stay connected—can be fun and add a face-to-face element to communication, forging stronger emotional connections
One-on-one virtual consultations	Create bespoke experiences that extend your brand's integration into your clients' lives
Interactive chatbots that use luxury language/tone	Ensure all interactions align with your brand's high standards, and make clients feel uniquely catered to
Personalized DM outreach on social media	Show appreciation and strengthen relationships
Curated social media content and tagging clients in tailored posts	Fosters a sense of recognition (inclusivity) and exclusivity
Custom digital invitations	When elegant and interactive, increase anticipation and excitement for events
Members-only portals with VIP access sections	Make clients feel special, encouraging loyalty and frequent engagement, especially luxury lovers

Analog Communication Methods

Handwritten notes	Hands-down one of my most favorite strategies—it demonstrates thoughtfulness and care, adding a personal touch that is memorable and cherished
High-end packaging for mailings	Enhances the unboxing experience and reinforces brand identity
Personalized phone calls	Lovely direct interactions with senior team members show clients their value and importance
Premium print invitations for events	Convey exclusivity and set a sophisticated tone
Personal concierge phone calls	Ensure high-touch, personalized service
Private event follow-ups	Solidify positive memories and deepen client connections
Personalized welcome kits	Set the stage for a long-lasting, valued client relationships
Tailored catalogs	Keep clients engaged by showcasing products relevant to their tastes
Special occasion mailings of cards or gifts	Acknowledge client milestones to build personal connections and loyalty
Surprise gift deliveries	When tailored to client preferences, enhance the relationship and demonstrate attention to detail—everyone will tell you this is another one of my favorite ways to delight clients and build advocates

Communication's Amuse-Bouche

An "amuse-bouche" is that small surprise, a savory bite you receive from the chef in some restaurants, before your meal. It is unexpected, serves to delight, and is a shortcut to patrons' attention and loyalty.

Did you see what I did there? I just used an attention-grabbing shortcut to communication: a metaphor. Using metaphors to simplify complex concepts and connect ideas will make your messaging even more engaging; these images are powerful and creative—and memorable and repeatable—ways to demonstrate your value. They create a visual image that lights up the brain's right hemisphere, making it easier to remember you. The right hemisphere of the brain allows us to understand context and engage with the world in a comprehensive way. Metaphors can shape how people see an idea; they can shift mindsets, point to a new solution, and show things in a new way. They are a great addition to your brand's storytelling toolkit, and they are especially helpful when inviting people to work with you—through sales conversations, presentations, and branding—in getting (and keeping) client and prospective-client attention.

Meeting planners and speaking bureau partners who find speakers for those meetings often call me the Energizer Bunny—a title I love, and if we've met, you know how accurate it is! Professionally, as a global keynote speaker, I am paid to bring energy and education to my clients and the audiences I serve in ballrooms and boardrooms, so this metaphor benefits my clients and makes me smile.

Similarly, I call the CEO of Associated Luxury Hotels International, Mike Dominguez, a sommelier. Why? ALHI is a global sales and marketing organization committed to the event and travel industry for meetings, incentives, conventions, and exhibitions. They connect hotels and resorts with meeting professionals to deliver personalized service and ensure successful programs. They pair the exact right hotel property with the exact right event professional for the perfect event, just like pairing a great wine with a great meal. So, voilà—a sommelier!

In another example, I refer to one of my clients, a chief operating officer at a hospital, as an air traffic controller. If you have ever watched a hospital drama on TV, you will understand why that rings true. One of my aviation CEO clients says she's like the pilot for her clients (and she's a pilot in real life, so that's fun). In each case, the metaphor helps you focus on the aspect of someone or something that feels most special, defining, or differentiated.

Here are some metaphors that might work for you. Try these or others on to see whether they are a good fit for you and what you do:

- The conductor of an orchestra creates beautiful music and has everyone playing off the same song sheet (can be used to indicate direction, focus, or collaboration)

- The GPS guides the way (can be used to demonstrate leadership, focus, and strategy)
- A Swiss Army knife (indicates your ability to handle any situation and creatively solve)
- A lighthouse (creates a safe path for people to navigate rough waters)
- AI (describes your ability to curate large amounts of information quickly)
- A detective (able to investigate all the options and provide a solution)

If you were a metaphor, what would you be? I ask this question of luxury leaders all the time! What is an excellent metaphor for your organization that quickly helps clients understand precisely what you do? Now your beautiful brain is working overtime to find yours, right? It is such a fun exercise.

Your challenge is to invite your team to brainstorm a list and choose the best one! Use the chosen metaphor in your sales conversations to differentiate your product. Ideating on metaphors is one of my favorite activities, so reach out to me if I can help your team with this!

CHAMPAGNE MOMENT

Let's find out your luxury mindset using our self-assessment. You can discover yours by investing less than five minutes to answer a few questions. Perhaps pour yourself a glass of your favorite sparkling beverage or make a coffee in your favorite mug to sip while you complete it. Once you do, you will receive a personalized email report. To learn more, visit the Luxury Mindset website (luxuryisamindset.com).

6

Elevating Experience

· · · · ·

The luxury lever *excite* asks you to create share-worthy experiences that tap into all five senses. When clients think of your brand, you want them to ask, with awe and wonder, "What else will they do?"

*Luxury is how you make
people feel and create lasting memories.*

Nancy Ebel
luxury travel advisor, Hill's Travel

Creating share-worthy experiences means crafting remarkable moments that clients are excited to tell others about—offering personalized touches to exceed expectations, delivering seamless experiences, and anticipating needs before they arise. Being share-worthy is about evoking emotion, especially surprise and delight—whether that is because of an unexpected upgrade, a bespoke thank-you gift, or a flawlessly orchestrated event. When clients feel genuinely seen, valued, and indulged, they become enthusiastic advocates, eager to share their extraordinary experiences with others.

What experiences do you create that cause clients to take out their phones and capture the moment to share it with their world?

Ann Handley, a world-class marketer and speaker, publishes a bi-weekly newsletter called *Total Annarchy*. It was born on January 28, 2018, and at the time of writing has over fifty thousand loyal and engaged subscribers, growing weekly. Every other Sunday morning, I make coffee, curl up in my favorite soft chair under a cozy cashmere blanket, and open my laptop, eager to read her entertaining, informative, fun newsletter. What makes Ann's newsletter so share-worthy is that it feels as if she is sitting having coffee with you and you are the only person she is writing to. Ann is a master storyteller who makes her readers feel seen. Her newsletters offer valuable advice and are filled with humor and metaphor. She makes her readers feel smart. Her ideas come to life with her conversational, practical approach, and people share the newsletter by forwarding the email, posting it on social media, including it in their slide decks on conference stages, and maybe, like me, writing about her in their book. I have always had a crush on Ann's brain; she's fun and has the coolest metric I have ever heard of for email marketing (that she invented, of course). It's called OWBR (open to write back rate). She will tell you it's pronounced "owe-burr."

How many people do you know who build their Sunday morning routine around reading a newsletter? Is your newsletter or email marketing strategy one that your subscribers anticipate with as much joy as Ann Handley's subscribers do? Is there a way you can help your readers feel seen or smarter or funnier because they read your brilliance, and then keenly await your next installment? Consider how any content you share is valuable to your clients and heightens their experiences (by talking about what matters to them). One tip is to avoid being a Braggosaurus Rex online (only talking about yourself/your brand).

You can also design spaces and little moments to make clients feel special, grab their attention, and inspire them to share. Maybe you curate a reception area that people want to capture for the 'Gram (as the kids say). Perhaps you can create moments of personal reveal. For example, a bakery might produce a custom cake and then offer to grandly open the box for the client while they capture a short video of it. Perhaps they might also film the baker talking about how much they enjoyed creating the masterpiece. A local coffee roaster might invite top-tier clients who purchase a subscription or gift set to an "experience day," where they can learn about coffee roasting, maybe even craft their own blend.

When all else fails, there is one thing that is sure to delight almost anyone into sharing. What do you think it is?

The Sweetest Sound—and Sight

As a kid, when you entered a retail store or gas station that had white metal stands filled with personalized items with names on them—key rings, rulers, pencils, and holiday decorations—did you scour the retail shelves searching for your name? Yep, same same. But mine was never there. What a disappointment! People love to see their names. When you see a group picture or an old school photo, do you look for yourself first? Yep, same same. We have trained our brain to look for our own face.

When joining Zoom or Microsoft Teams calls, I often change my name to "Neen—fan of [insert client's name here]." It takes less than five seconds to personalize it, and it always makes them laugh! It is a no-cost, fun touchpoint that makes people feel special.

In his brilliant book *How to Win Friends and Influence People*, Dale Carnegie wrote, "A person's name is the sweetest sound." I would add that sharing a person's name is the sweetest sight! People love it when you customize for them, and if you can make them smile, it is often share-worthy! Other ways you might personalize for your clients, in person and online, include:

- providing monogramming on special products associated with your service
- engraving a client gift
- sending a handwritten card of appreciation
- giving a gift with a purchase, based on their buying habits
- printing customized product labels
- allowing color customization and choices
- embossing products

Louis Vuitton retail stores in major cities offer complimentary hot-stamping initials on bags, luggage tags, and travel stamps in passport holders. Department stores and online retailers often allow monograms for home products, personal goods, and travel items. Some shoe manufacturers allow you to add names and color choices. In fact, many companies personalize items, including Coca-Cola, M&Ms, YETI, L.L.Bean, Pottery Barn, Converse, and even Build-A-Bear! Of course, you can also leverage online specialists on platforms like Etsy that represent small businesses.

Engage the Senses

Antoine Arnault, CEO of Christian Dior and board member of Louis Vuitton Moët Hennessy (LVMH), says, "Luxury is about pleasing the senses and the soul. It's about creating products that can be personal, special, and perfectly tailored to one's desires."

Part of this system of elevation is to find ways to incorporate the experience of all five senses into your clients' journey with you. At product design sessions, challenge your team to ideate on all the ways you can appeal to sight, touch, hearing, taste, and smell. And add this requirement to your internal checklists for creation of new releases. In debrief meetings after a product launch, ask the team to identify any additional opportunities to engage the senses. In your client focus groups or client feedback sessions, include questions that will help you understand if additional senses could be appealed to.

Consider how IKEA leverages all five senses in its shopping experience. Thoughtfully designed showrooms help customers envision furniture in their homes (sight). Subtle background music makes the shopping experience

Great experiences
delight two of
our senses. Elevated
experiences delight
all five and create an
emotional connection
to your brand.

· · · · ·

calming and inviting (sound). By encouraging hands-on exploration of furniture, fabrics, and accessories in-store, the store appeals to sight and touch. The popular store's famous Swedish meatballs, lingonberry jam, and other signature foods at IKEA restaurants (taste) and that special aroma of freshly baked cinnamon rolls (smell) in the food court complement the overall shopping experience. IKEA could just have a marketplace, but it knows its multisensory formula works. A regular furniture-shopping trip becomes a full sensory experience that invites exploration and leads customers to spend a longer time in the store. And did you know that, according to Alan Penn, a professor at University College London Bartlett School, 60 percent of purchases made at IKEA are unplanned? Engaging the five senses could be a very profitable strategy for your business.

Leveraging all five senses increases emotional connection to your brand. At the famous historic Hôtel Barrière Le Majestic in Cannes, France, while I was there for a speaking engagement in December, my client Virtuoso hosted a special event with their head sommelier. It was a custom cocktail-making class. The room was festive, with elaborate and elegant holiday decorations and instrumental Christmas music playing in the background. Every guest was in awe of the beauty of the room. When they entered they were handed a small, soft, white organza bag containing a bottle of fragrance. Later, during the class, we sprayed that fragrance over the top of a crystal cocktail glass to enhance the tasting experience. While many times I've seen stores spray fragrance on your wrist to test a new scent, I had never before seen someone spritz a cocktail this way! Such a delightful experience and a fun example of how to uplift even a drink, through smell, taste, sight, sound, and touch. During the lesson, I noticed the room smelled like citrus and watched everyone smiling, sipping their cocktail thoughtfully. We were also delighted to take the fragrance home to share with our loved ones.

Let's take a moment to delight in each of the senses.

Smell: Our sense of smell, olfactory, is one of our most heightened senses, and it is deeply connected to exceptional experiences. A scent can transport us to memories of our childhood or of someone special. Many hotels employ a "nose" to create destination-inspired perfumes. This is called scentscaping. And yes, a nose is a real job—google it. Next time you are in a hotel lobby, take a deep breath and notice if you can detect a signature scent. Often, in luxury hotel gift stores, you can purchase that scent or related bath products to remind you of your travels and, specifically, of your stay at the hotel. EDITION Hotels is one of my favorite scents, regardless of if I am in Tampa, New York, or Madrid. Their signature scent transports me to memories of stays in their gorgeous properties around the globe.

What smell makes you smile? That fresh scent after a rain shower? Fresh-cut grass? Red wine in a glass? An easy elevation strategy is to add a custom scent to your lobby or office so that clients associate it with you. But remember, it needs to be subtle and not overwhelming. Too much of a good thing, or a poorly crafted smell, may turn clients off. You don't want that.

Sight and Taste: Luxury hotels often offer fruit waters in their lobby to quench your thirst; the fruit happily bobbing in the water inspires you to treat yourself. Having fruit-infused water on display could be an easy addition to business common areas. Instead of stale wrapped candy that collects dust in a bowl, could you offer fresh fruit as an alternative? Think about what that simple switch indicates: you can't leave fresh fruit out for days, so it is another small luxury touch that shows you are paying attention to all the small details.

Touch: You can amplify the emotional connection and sensory experience, especially with touch, through the paper stock you choose for your business cards and thank-you notes, or the packaging materials that surround your products or services. Or even the furniture. Have you ever noticed the velvet stools in champagne bars or the marble countertops in regular bars? Have you experienced retailers encouraging you to try on the jewelry? Have you noticed that some credit card companies choose an exceptionally substantial plastic or even metal to make their cards feel different in your hands? Financial services invest in higher-grade paper stock for materials; this helps make their intangible product of knowledge and advice into a tangible experience for their clientele. When working with sustainable companies, have you noticed they use environmentally friendly recycled paper to be consistent with their brands?

Sound: Reminiscing combines an emotional connection with a memory. Have you ever heard a song on the radio, and it instantly transports you back to a time in your life when that song meant something to you? Do you hear a theme song of your favorite childhood TV show, and you know all the words and are transported back to running home from school to turn on the TV just in time to watch, say, the Fonz on *Happy Days*? Nostalgia is a brilliant strategy to connect in a deeper way and to spark delight in your clients. I saw Associated Luxury Hotels International use this strategy brilliantly in its events in the music selection, ice-breaker activities, slide presentations, and even event themes. Mike Dominguez, the company's CEO, shared that "nostalgia is back," and it made me smile. What music could you incorporate in your business to transport people? What themes could you incorporate into your meetings and events that would bring joy to your guests? What candy or snacks would instantly remind people of their childhood?

Could you create a deeper emotional connection by adding theater to engage more of your clients' senses, so they want to share your brand with others?

Inclusivity

Brands that tailor for diverse needs get my attention. I have always appreciated how financial services brands like Bank of America and Starbucks provide braille accessible products for anyone who might need them and focus on tactile experiences. Rubbermaid specifically designs ergonomic cleaning products for ease and efficiency, especially for people who use their products for long hours.

Having a diverse group of friends and family, I notice businesses that provide even more exceptional experiences that are inclusive, thoughtful, and discreet. Wheelchair access, larger-font materials, options for allergies, representation in printed materials and advertising, braille, accessible websites, hearing loops and other technologies for people who are hard of hearing, language interpretations, and translations are all ways brands can create more accessibility for their clients. The more brands do this, the more they will be referred to by others, especially in communities that notice the customization.

One of my favorite clients, the Comcast Local Media Development team, created the first sensory-friendly room in Philadelphia that is open to the public. It features a multisensory environment that is calming with sensory stimulation that caters to a diversity of sensory needs, equipped with features like color-changing floor tiles, a visual infinity wall, and even sensory rocking chairs!

In elevating the experiences clients have of you, also consider how you are appealing to diverse ages, cultures, and generations. I sometimes think about how to deliver the message or experience if a person were eight, eighteen, thirty-eight, fifty-eight, or eighty-eight. This simple system allows me to consider a wide range of viewpoints, popular and cultural references, and learning styles.

Being Australian (and also an American citizen), I often like to question whether the offering is considerate of a diversity of cultural differences. This might include analyzing the visuals in marketing materials, PowerPoint slide decks, social media posts, and website designs. It could also involve examining messages to make sure the words used don't mean something else in other cultures. I was once hired by a very conservative, major financial services brand because they "couldn't understand why their Australian offices were not embracing their latest marketing campaign." The team refused to wear all the logo merchandise they had shipped Down Under. When I asked them about the campaign, they replied, "It's so clever, Neen. It is 'Root for your client.'" That might seem harmless to you as you read it, but did you know that the word "root" in Aussie slang means sex?! Do I hear you laughing? I certainly did when they told me, and they were mortified! Do your homework and test the images, language, messages, and colors with a variety of sources to allow you to deliver a better experience for everyone.

Systemized Thoughtfulness

When you turn positive intentions into practical actions, you demonstrate that you care. When people feel cared for, they are more likely to engage and to engage for longer. You can make your clients feel cared for too. Knowing they are valued beyond their transactions will deepen their loyalty to you, which is important because relationship drives revenue. The deeper the relationship, the more you are top of mind for your clients (mind share). We also know that repeatable execution leads to repeatable results. So, how do you teach kindness, curiosity, and thoughtfulness? How do you make that repeatable? You use systemized thoughtfulness. Systemized thoughtfulness is the practice of intentionally building systems and processes into your daily routine to be actively mindful and considerate toward others, essentially making thoughtful actions a consistent and structured part of your interactions, rather than relying on spontaneous gestures alone.

This technique transforms thoughtful gestures into a repeatable artform. With systemized thoughtfulness, you create a process to stay connected with the clients you want to become your advocates. You can start by choosing the top twenty clients you want to stay connected with, and brainstorm different ways to connect monthly. I keep a simple Google spreadsheet (so I can share it with my team) and make an appointment with myself on the first Monday of each month where I sit down with the spreadsheet and brainstorm a unique, creative way to connect. Sometimes I send a book or book recommendation, create a personalized video message, mail a handwritten note, or recommend an inspiring TED Talk. I might send a magazine like *Virtuoso* or *Beyond the Meeting Room* to clients in travel and hospitality industries who will enjoy this quality content. I challenge myself to personalize every touchpoint.

Sally Turner, director of sales for 360 Private Travel, trains her team to combine personal high-touch experience with seamless service. She empowers her team, encouraging them to personalize every client experience and demonstrate empathy. One touching example is a long-time client who, having lost her spouse, planned a trip. But she was procrastinating about packing because she was feeling sad and lonely. The travel advisor went to her house to help her pack and ensure she had everything she needed for the trip. Sally's team turned a difficult experience into a caring and supportive moment.

There are endless possibilities for how you might systemize thoughtfulness. The sanitation service in our neighborhood knows one of the homes has an elderly couple, so they drag their emptied recycling and trash cans back up the drive to make it easier for them. This act is so kind. Every holiday season we fill a basket with water, Gatorade, and snacks and leave it on our front porch with a sign encouraging the delivery service and post office drivers who come to our home to take whatever they need. This small gesture, during their busiest season, is appreciated by many, and several of my neighbors implement it too, which makes me so happy! When I shared this tradition on social media many years ago, other people committed to do the same. This little thing is the least we can do to make other people's lives easier, and it makes me wonder: What can we do to practice thoughtfulness in our own backyard, in our neighborhood, and for our clients? Tiny acts of kindness have a ripple effect in people's lives that you may never see.

Exciting people about your brand isn't enough. Capturing their attention is fun, as is the knowledge that they want to progress further in their journey with you, tell others about you, and even share online. For brands focused on creating advocates, though, the next step is to engage the lever of *delight*.

CHAMPAGNE MOMENT

If you want to treat your senses to a little luxury this week, try this: buy yourself flowers. Yes, really! Pop in to a florist today and pick up a bouquet for your desk at the office, for your reception desk, or to take home with you. Each time you notice them, take in the smell of the flowers, enjoy the colors you see, take note of the textures of the petals, and remind yourself that this small, thoughtful action makes the space feel and smell more beautiful and it is something that can be enjoyed by others too. If flowers aren't your thing, what about a decadent box of chocolates? You don't like chocolate? How can we be friends?! Just kidding!

# 7

Inspiring Experience

· · · · ·

With the luxury lever *delight*, you pay personalized attention, offer exceptional service, and add value to offerings that will spark delight and leave your clients asking, "How did they anticipate needs I didn't even know I had?"

Luxury is the ability to craft unique, personalized experiences that exceed clients' expectations. Our commitment is to make each client feel special, ensuring they leave with a sense of extraordinary value and unforgettable memories.

Andrea Grisdale
CEO and founder, Italy Connection Bellagio

Poet Elizabeth Bibesco said: "Blessed are those who can give without remembering and receive without forgetting." This emphasis on the importance of giving generously without expecting anything in return, while also remembering to be grateful for the kindness received, is a great reminder to all of us.

We can all learn from luxury brands that consciously distinguish the way they give gifts. They don't wait until the holidays, and they are strategic in considering other opportunities—for example, when a client achieves a milestone with them, moves into a new home, or has a new family (or furry) member. And no, I am not talking about your branded swag. That is not a gift. That is marketing.

John Ruhlin, author of *Giftology*, recommends gifting to surprise clients and says, "Gifts are symbols of the value you place on the relationship." I like that; it makes a client's experience with you tangible. A friend of ours works with John's company to provide customized, engraved items to clients and friends. When my husband, Andy, bought his first boat, *No Worries* (an Aussie expression meaning "everything will be okay"), our friend sent him useful boating items engraved with the boat's name.

John also says, "Remember: It's not the thought that counts, but it's the thoughtful thought that counts." This makes me think of one of the best gifts I ever received. It was from my sister, Deb. I had damaged my silver charm bracelet by stupidly wearing it in a hot tub and every charm had tarnished. I'd been collecting individual charms since I was a pre-teen, and one day, it went missing. I was so sad thinking that I'd lost it. But in fact, Deb had taken it and carefully and painstakingly hand-polished every tiny charm. Then she wrapped it up and gave it to me in a perfect package. I cried when I opened it; to this day, it is one of the most thoughtful gifts I have ever received.

Imagine my delight opening the book launch package from customer experience speaker (and my friend) Joey Coleman. What made this gift unique and strategic was his use of LEGO. Not only did he send me a signed, personalized copy of his book *Never Lose an Employee Again*, but he also included a custom LEGO figure of me, complete with blonde hair and blue eyes, standing on a stage with a microphone! This level of customization and personalization was a touching and fun gesture, and every time I see that mini-figure I think fondly of Joey and the impact of the work he does in the world. It's also a reminder for me to recommend him to meeting planners who want a great keynote speaker—mind share and market share!

Show Me You Know Me

Caroline Huo, known for redefining the luxury experience in luxury real estate, has a famous mantra, "Show me you know me." This brilliant phrase (which she attributes to thought leader Phil Jones, author of the book *Exactly What to Say*) is one of the core beliefs in her business, and it is embedded in the team philosophy. Caroline's team is constantly winning awards and continues to grow year over year. "Excellence always in all ways," she says. Caroline is also famous for her legendary personalized gifting strategy.

One of her clients, a Hermès lover with significant wealth (who could have purchased anything she wanted), purchased a home through Caroline. Instead of gifting her yet another Hermès scarf, Caroline exceeded her expectations beyond measure. She knew her client longed for the bread she missed from her Midwest hometown. So she secretly sourced locally milled flour and the recipe for the bread. When she presented this gift to her client (who already had everything you could want), she was deeply moved, and these feelings deepened Caroline's connection with her client. Now, that's thoughtful!

And if you think that's impressive, let me share another amazing example of Caroline's thoughtfulness. One of her clients, a recent widow, was selling her house to move to an assisted living facility. When asked what she would miss the most about the home she had shared with her husband of many years, she mentioned her lemon tree—a tree they had had through their marriage and many home moves.

When Caroline's team sold her home, as a parting gift, they delivered to her new home a lemon tree branch that had been grafted from the original tree, so that she would forever have that tree with her. Are you teary reading that? Yeah, me too, when I first heard this story.

A potential client once mentioned to me that he loved to go fly-fishing with his grandson... Now, if we have met, it won't take you long to realize that I don't know the first thing about fly-fishing! So I bought a subscription for him, and that six-dollar magazine subscription started arriving on his desk each month. By the third issue, he reached out to me and said, "Neen, I love how you paid attention to our conversation; let's talk about you working with my executive team for our next strategic planning event." Magazine subscriptions are an easy, low-cost, systemized gift to show potential and existing clients that you see them. And once you subscribe, it shows up on their desk as a monthly reminder that they are important to you. You might be thinking, "I could never remember those kinds of details!" Perhaps that's true, but what if you leveraged a client management system to capture that information, just like restaurants and hotels use their reservation systems to record notes about their diners and guests so they can delight them on their next visit?

When designing your gifting strategy, be conscious of your industry rules or company guidelines, and carefully choose brands that are congruent with your values and beliefs. Remember, the key is personalization. Just like my wonderful experience at Fairmont Tremblant

Strategic mentoring
cultivates confident
professionals
who delight clients
with exceptional
experiences.

· · · · ·

with the Canada Goose jacket that felt so customized and personalized!

Upskilling a Team That Delights

When you upskill and invest in your team members, they deliver even more powerful, personalized experiences to your clients, who then invest in your business. Mentoring is a win-win-win for everyone! Strategic mentoring cultivates a team of confident, capable professionals who feel empowered to delight clients with exceptional bespoke experiences. You might consider establishing guidelines about ways your mentees can feel empowered to delight your clients, even assigning budgets they can use for that purpose, as The Ritz-Carlton does. Employees of the luxury hotel chain are given a budget and are empowered to use it to enhance a guest experience without seeking management approval. Managers trust their team to make the right decisions.

An easy way to start a mentoring system is to make a list of your top high-potential talent to develop, and then meet with them to assess their needs and how they might like to be mentored. Share your list with your human resources leader, if you have one, so they know this level of informal development is occurring. At your first mentoring meeting, create an agenda to understand their desired outcomes and an agreement for how you want to work together. Then give them an assignment.

When I worked in corporate, a fun assignment I always gave my team (and something easy for you to try) was to suggest they mystery-shop an organization, maybe even a competitor. Mystery-shopping does not have to be complicated. It is just a system for your mentees to notice how they were treated, how they felt. Invite them to document what they loved and disliked, and to make recommendations for what your organization could do to enhance the overall experience. Ask them to share their observations with you in a one-on-one meeting and possibly in your team meeting. If your business is large enough, this exercise can be extended to mystery-shopping your own brand.

A system my team and I use with our top-tier clients is to imagine we are a user of our keynote speeches and executive coaching. As a team, we walk through every tiny detail from the first inquiry via our website, or by phone, email, or social media, and then track it all the way through to the time onsite for the keynote, travel arrangements, meeting all the crew, the AV tech check, liaising with housekeeping, client meetings, and audience interactions. We review any materials, templates, automated emails, invoices, and printed materials shared with clients. We consider travel, logistics, printing, and even outfits. And then, after the event is over, we consider every interaction and touchpoint to question if it feels like a luxury experience. If not, what can we do to make sure no details are overlooked?

This is why I encourage hoteliers to sleep in their hotel rooms, insurance brokers to see how it feels to make a claim, realtors to visit other open houses, performers to watch plays and movies and attend musicals, teachers to be students, retailers to be shoppers, travel advisors to be tourists, and chauffeurs to be driven. Think about the last time you experienced what you do with the lens of how your top-tier clients would experience you. Are there small tweaks you could make, annoying pain points to be eliminated, forms to be automated, process redundancies that could be removed? Experiencing your own products gives you new insights and might spark fresh ideas to enhance them.

Through our journey together exploring luxury mindsets, we've discovered how systems of elevation, combined with meticulous attention to detail, create moments that matter. Now let's transform these insights into action by exploring how to ignite your clients' passion and turn your clients into your most powerful advocates.

CHAMPAGNE MOMENT

There is so much conversation lately about the right glassware for champagne (flute versus universal glass). My friend Meg loves to serve champagne in an old-fashioned coupe. There is something so glamorous, so elegant about holding a coupe. It adds a little drama, and it's a little indulgent. This week, could you pour yourself your favorite bubbles (champagne or something else sparkling) into a fabulous glass?

8

Leveraging Experience

· · · · ·

When you build loyalty and trust, you encourage your clients to become passionate advocates who promote your brand and attract other clients to you. This is the luxury lever *ignite*. When you provide exceptional experiences, people ask, "Who else can I tell about my experience?"

Luxury is about the experience of excellence, craftsmanship, and thoughtful execution that elevates something from ordinary to extraordinary.

Gina Lyons
CEO, A Vine Affair

This luxury lever of *ignite*, where you create advocates, feels like a full-circle attention moment. Here's what I mean by that: When you begin to engage the Experience Elevation Model, you focus on how to attract the attention of potential (and existing) clients by enticing them with fresh and appealing storytelling. You invite them, by speaking the language they want to hear, into experiences that make them feel special. And then you excite them, inspiring them because they are a part of something special and you offer them even more levels of access. To delight them, you anticipate needs they didn't even know they had. Now, this stage of *ignite* is where you really leverage all the work you've done to build transformational relationships with your clients.

With this lever, you move the mind share you've gained by engaging the other four luxury levers to leverage market share; your clients become passionate advocates who draw others to you and who keep returning for more. You focus energy on engaging happy clients who spread the message about your brand.

Brittany Hodak, customer experience speaker and author of *Creating Superfans*, says, "When you say that you're great, it's marketing; when *other* people say that you're great, it's magic." I agree! This short, powerful statement is also a reminder to invest in finding out what your clients want and need, and what they say about you. Investing time and attention to capture this information will allow you to provide transformational, magical experiences and lasting memories.

Make People Feel Seen, Heard, and Valued

I am curious about how to teach curiosity. Perhaps we can agree that being curious about how to make your clients' personal or professional lives better will make them feel seen, heard, and valued. Remember, luxury is about experiences, not things. Leveraging luxury is not necessarily about selling high-priced goods or services; it is about how you consistently deliver value, build strong relationships, and actively engage clients in your brand journey. It's all about relationships.

The Ritz-Carlton Hotel Company, founded in 1983, is one of the best examples of this approach, and I've always admired the company's philosophy of anticipatory service. When I first met Herve Humler, cofounder of The Ritz-Carlton Hotel Company, I was awestruck. Like a giddy teenage girl meeting her crush, I blurted out, "Ritz-Carlton, personalization at its finest!" He smiled warmly, sharing that the philosophy of genuinely taking care of people has served the company well and established it as a true luxury leader. His vision for luxury service has made a massive impact in the world, elevating the standard of luxury hotels.

Renowned for its commitment to creating personalized and memorable guest experiences, The Ritz-Carlton's success in ensuring that each interaction—in person, online, or on the phone—feels tailored is a result of its meticulous systems, empowered team culture, and adherence to its founders' philosophy and three steps of service: that each guest is to be greeted warmly, that their needs should be anticipated and fulfilled, and that they should be given a fond farewell. It has systemized its hiring process by seeking out individuals who naturally align with The Ritz-Carlton's values for respect, elegance, and world-class service. The company hires for attitude and trains for skill using competency-based evaluation techniques. Its training programs are world-renowned, and many industries outside luxury have implemented its practices. (Remember High Point University from chapter 2? They use The Ritz-Carlton's training principles on their campus.)

Every team member at The Ritz-Carlton carries a credo card outlining the company's mission and values. In daily briefings, to inspire others, they share exceptional experiences they have created, and they focus on storytelling. The company keeps detailed notes in its Customer Relationship Management system about its guests and leverages the data for hyper-personalization of guest stays.

What has always impressed me with The Ritz-Carlton, a lesson to every one of us in business, is its preemptive service. Employees try to anticipate guest needs before they ask. They do this before a guest arrives, through deep listening in calls, and also while guests are staying onsite. They pay close attention to requests, conversations, and comments to plan how they can surprise and delight. And finally, they embed this philosophy in every department, with every team member, regardless of whether they are front of house or back of house. This is just another reason they are often held up as the platinum standard of luxury service.

The result is that guests of The Ritz-Carlton feel seen, heard, and valued, the way they would in any good relationship.

From Satisfied Clients to Vocal Advocates

You can harness testimonials, networking, and word-of-mouth to build credibility, attract attention, and become top of mind as the go-to solution in your industry by turning highly satisfied clients into vocal advocates.

Testimonials are a way to showcase authentic stories from your happy clients. Highlight specific results or transformations they've experienced, and present these stories as videos, written quotes, or case studies. Strategically place testimonials on your website and in social media and marketing materials. This is what the marketing kids call "social proof," and when a client provides it for you (rather than you saying it about yourself), it is so powerful. I am a massive fan of video testimonials! Hearing the tone and seeing faces gives the message more impact.

Networking is about forging meaningful relationships with industry peers and clients. Attending events, joining associations, and hosting exclusive gatherings can have meaningful return on investment (ROI). When either your brand is known as a connector, or you are known as a leader who introduces people to valuable contacts, it builds goodwill and positions your business as a trusted resource, once again helping you stay top of mind.

If you want to encourage satisfied clients to share their experiences, you must create moments worthy of word-of-mouth promotion. Surprise your clients with unexpected delights—personalized notes, exclusive perks, or follow-up touches after purchases. The Avery Bar at The Ritz-Carlton Boston used to hand out wooden drink coasters to certain customers; it was a way of making their regular clients feel more special that elevated their experience at the hotel. Do not expect people to speak about processes and procedures that feel like a normal way of operating. We have talked about many share-worthy types of experiences in this book; by now, I hope you are working on some for your clients and prospective clients. So, just a tip: Make sharing enticing by offering referral incentives and creating a branded hashtag for social media engagement.

Advocacy comes from building long-term relationships, where people feel valued and part of something greater. They need to trust you.

But the effort does not stop there.

Once you do transform clients into advocates, you need to keep paying attention to them, acknowledging their contribution to your business and putting systems in place to thank them, especially when they refer others to you. Andrea Grisdale, CEO of IC Bellagio (Italy Connection Bellagio), often gives shout-outs to people on social media. Tagging them with social recognition highlights great teamwork, builds morale, and strengthens the client relationship. In her experience, when you are "trustworthy and transparent with your clients they become advocates." When her company had its twenty-fifth anniversary, she hosted the who's who of the luxury travel industry to descend on Bellagio, Italy. There she showcased local partners in a sustainable and glamorous anniversary event, thanking all those who had advocated for her company all these years. She was the talk of the season (or the talk of the Ton, if you are a *Bridgerton* fan).

When you begin planning how you will show your ongoing appreciation of your advocates, think BIG. Did you know that for a ridiculous price you can customize the playlist of the famous Bellagio Fountains in Las Vegas? You could also book a table for two in the middle of the Bellagio Conservatory at night. Yes, seriously. These ridiculously extravagant experiences might require significant investment, but perhaps they inspire you to think about something your business could do that is so exclusive and so share-worthy that you could offer it to your top advocates? Think creatively, ridiculously, without boundaries or budgets. List all your wild ideas, and then reality-check for options that are possible within your constraints.

Be strategic about how your efforts to appreciate advocates could also serve to attract new clients or benefit a partner. Several times a year, I curate exclusive events and invite my top clients and friends, giving them access to a private shopping experience outside retail store hours at some of my clients' and partners' spaces, for example, Louis Vuitton, Chanel, and Tiffany & Co. The result for the stores is often new clientele, while I have achieved a wonderful way to thank my clients and develop stronger relationships with them. Yet another benefit of these invitation-only events is that, although the invitees may not know each other at first, they meet and expand their own networks of like-minded people in an intimate environment. Many often want to bring a friend too, so I get to meet some of the people who are important to them. Everyone wins! When is the last time you hosted your best clients to thank them for their business? Could you invite them to join you at an event or a conference?

Exclusive Events to Build Advocates

As a regular keynote speaker and consultant for Associated Luxury Hotels International, I am in awe of the deliberate way ALIII builds genuine, long-term relationships that naturally create advocates for the association, by focusing on authentic interactions rather than pushing for fandom. ALHI exemplifies how to cultivate advocates by crafting exclusive, invitation-only events—over eighty across the globe—that strengthen connections among hoteliers, clients, and industry professionals. These events go beyond networking, incorporating thought leadership, education, and curated experiences that appeal to ALHI's loyal advocates.

The event design offers a luxurious experience, from gifting stations at check-in and thoughtful amenities, to customized agendas that balance networking, downtime, and experiential activities. ALHI designs event agendas with "white space," so their busy guests also have fun and downtime to process their experiences—something that is not often planned for. They also organize sessions for peer-to-peer learning, so that the industry keeps raising its standards. This is something the company is known (and appreciated) for.

Mike Dominguez, ALHI CEO, says, "We are working with busy executives and understand that, because time is such a precious commodity, for anyone to say yes to our events, we know they attend because of the relationship we have." In other words, people attend ALHI events because they are already in a relationship with ALHI. The events are not an attraction strategy—they are a deliberate, thoughtful retention strategy.

Mike believes that advocacy is a by-product of taking care of people in ways they are not accustomed to. Providing exceptional care leads to loyalty. ALHI events deliver

Being seen, heard, and valued: that's the exceptional experience.

.....

stress-free experiences and consistently add value to clients' lives in authentic, meaningful ways. I value their attention to detail and the red-carpet atmosphere they create. Each aspect, from tailored invitations and interactive event apps, to thoughtful menus and professionally curated gifting, underscores ALHI's commitment to delivering a luxury experience. Under Mike's leadership, ALHI treats every participant as a VIP, ensuring that all hoteliers, speakers, sponsors, and guests feel valued. This dedication to excellence fosters a sense of loyalty and advocacy that keeps ALHI events at the forefront of the luxury hotel industry.

Develop BDA in Your DNA

For over twenty years in my business, we have leveraged a system called BDA (before, during, after). We use BDA to customize keynotes for clients, elevate executive coaching assignments, and assist with the consulting we do for luxury and legacy brands. We developed a checklist of activities and questions we cover before, during, and after our client interactions. We even include the checklist in our speaking proposals to show clients the depth of our pre- and post-event work.

My job as a keynote speaker is to make it look really easy on stage—seamless for the client, and entertaining and engaging for the audience. To do that requires hundreds of hours in pre-reading client materials; learning their KPIs, acronyms, and challenges; customizing my speeches;

sharing marketing materials and custom videos for their audience; interviewing key stakeholders (including board members, frontline workers, leadership, and sometimes clients); and curating all the information to deliver a customized keynote. During the high-energy event, I include their content, solutions for their challenges, and audience interaction—all designed so I look like I am part of their team. But it doesn't stop once I get off stage. We offer follow-up resources, additional marketing activations and accountability videos, and a debrief call. My team and I outline all the steps to provide a customized experience in a systemized way.

What is your version of BDA? What could you do to list all of the unique activities and activations you do before, during, and after your client interactions to make them feel more personalized? How can you let your clients know, so that they appreciate you even more and want to refer others to you?

Wired to Be Advocates

Do you have a favorite restaurant that you recommend to everyone who visits your city? Do you know someone who has a "guy" for everything? You know what I am talking about—those people who always have someone in their network to refer you to when you ask for something like, "Do you know a great painter?" You ask them, because you know they do.

Some people are just wired to be advocates. Once you understand the clients that really enjoy your products and services, explore how you can find more of that type of client. They themselves are a good source of referrals. You might ask them why they like doing business with you and if they are willing to share that appreciation with others.

Of the four types of luxury mindsets, luxury lovers inherently believe they are worth it. These folks are quick to decide about luxury experiences. Once they make up their mind, it is hard to change it. Research shows that they make the best brand advocates, as they love to tell the world about their experience and how a brand makes them feel. Your sales team needs to understand this. Also worth noting is that, when it comes to investing and making a decision, luxury lovers are the most influential over the other three mindsets. They can guide the reluctant and removed, who do not view luxury as a priority, showing them how the offering will save them time and hassle. Luxury lovers align with the confident and content mindset when they explain that it is worth investing to create memories for people they care about. For the pro prioritizer, any messaging that describes how luxury can be used for career and reputation will influence the conversation.

Our research showed that, once luxury lovers are impressed with a brand that provides a great offering, especially if they are given behind-the-scenes, exclusive access treatment, they want to tell everyone they know. They will actively post on social media, make personal recommendations and introductions, and mention your company and offering in their personal and professional lives.

So, finding more people who think like a luxury lover will be good for your business. The first place to start is with existing clients who are engaged with your brand. Ask them who they know that you need to know, and whether you can do anything to support them when they talk about your brand. Ask what tools might make it easier for them to share about you in conversations or on social media, so that they feel an even deeper sense of loyalty to you and want to help you grow your business.

Luxury lovers also enjoy knowing the inside scoop on product launches and having access to dedicated resources. So, introduce them to dedicated account managers or liaisons that can fast-track conversations and referrals, and share updates with them before you tell others. Ask these invested clients to share the news with their networks.

Human nature is that we love to be associated with success, so when someone trustworthy endorses a product or service, others are more likely to accept their recommendation and buy it too.

"Luxury is about the experience of excellence, craftsmanship, and thoughtful execution that elevates something from ordinary to extraordinary. Luxury gives a sense of exclusivity and indulgence and often taps into an emotional connection. It can be simple or grand, but it always feels special, whether it's found in a beautifully crafted bottle of vintage champagne, a serene five-star getaway, or even in a moment of peace and comfort that feels deeply personal," says Gina Lyons, CEO of A Vine Affair.

As a brand advocate for many champagne maisons, Gina has intimate knowledge of the Champagne region and deep relationships with the winemakers. Her access is unparalleled. I participated in a private tour of Champagne and stayed at the Royal Champagne Hotel with her. During our tour, we had dinner with families in their homes, visited private cellars of well-known growers, toured maisons never otherwise open to the public, sampled vintage champagnes not offered in the market, and attended exclusive events like Soirée Blanche, the best party in Champagne. It felt like a dream. Guests on her trips share widely on social media, provide testimonials, and often book additional trips with her. They all advocate for her and her company in their private and professional circles.

Gina is genuine and approaches her clients thoughtfully, by getting to know their needs and creatively anticipating what makes them feel valued. She helps clients build relationships with fine wine and champagne. She knows their palates and the experiences they enjoy, allowing her to propose opportunities they will love. Her goal is to surprise and delight clients with experiences of wine that will always excite them, and she constantly exceeds their expectations. That is why her Champagne trips sell out—often before the dates are even published.

Educate for Referrals

Almost every client highlighted in this book shared that word-of-mouth referral was their number-one strategy for attracting top-tier clients. Because my clients create such exceptional experiences, their clients want to refer others to them, and that ultimately drives revenue.

An important consideration to create advocates in your business is how to educate clients on giving your business referrals. Are you communicating about your organization and offerings with specific language that will help them? Do you tell your top-tier clients the types of clients you would like to work with who would be perfect referrals for you? If not, this is your gentle reminder, dear reader, to start asking for referrals from existing clients today. Don't be scared to ask. If they love your brand, they'll happily refer others to you.

Asking for business referrals is an art that every leader can master, and it requires a system so that you can make it a consistent practice. Start by identifying your most satisfied clients—those who have experienced measurable value from your services. Make a note in your CRM system's client notes, with a specific word or label your team can use, so you can go back and refer to those notes in future.

Share your genuine gratitude for their partnership through a handwritten note, email, phone call, or voice message. You might like to save the scripts you write in your system, so you can reuse them and tailor versions for future communications with other clients.

Then invite your satisfied clients' assistance in spreading the word about how they have enjoyed working with you, and share that you want to grow your business and work with more people like them. Use language like, "I'd love to help others like you. Who do you know that might benefit from what we've done together?" Ask confidently and with curiosity, not pressure.

Make the process simple by offering to follow up directly or providing shareable resources like a testimonial template or introduction email they might like to send on your behalf. By making it super easy and showing appreciation, you can transform happy clients into enthusiastic advocates.

I think the simplest system is to ask! People want to help you. Sometimes they just don't know how. So make it simple for them.

Surround Their Lifestyle

Bruce White, CEO of Johnson, Kendall & Johnson (JKJ), a full-service insurance broker and risk management firm, has the most powerful client attraction strategy. His genuine concern for delivering exceptional service is his passion and energy. "The best way to deepen relationships with top-tier clients is to surround their entire lifestyle," he says.

Building advocates is so much more than just "selling a product"—to surround a lifestyle is to become part of how your clients live, work, play, and express themselves. Think of tech companies that provide hardware (phones, laptops), software (cloud-based apps), and accessories (earphones and watches), all designed to interconnect and enhance their clients' life across personal, professional, and recreational activities. I love the phrase "surrounding their entire lifestyle," as it emphasizes holistic engagement and creating value.

Clients feel Bruce's enthusiasm and dedication, even during virtual meetings. This energy is paired with empathy and a genuine concern for his clients. Because they feel his sincerity, he notes, it is easy to "ask clients many times, Do you mind being a reference for us at JKJ?" Knowing that it will serve potential clients best if they hear directly from satisfied customers also creates more ease in asking for referrals.

Something else that will help in asking your top-tier clients for their referrals is contagious confidence.

Contagious Confidence

You know I changed schools a few times, and as the new kid, I had to develop contagious confidence. I've always walked into every room with the assumption that everyone wanted to play with me. That confidence level is contagious. It allows you to make everyone feel included, to act like the "hostess with the mostest" at a party (I am pretty sure this is in my DNA, from my social butterfly mum). It is that confidence that allows you to educate clients about referrals and make the ask. But you don't have to be born with it. It's a skill you develop.

As a leader, your ability to demonstrate confidence will be contagious to your team. They will feel reassured and confident in your product and service, which will show up in how they take care of your clients. When your team feels supported, trusts you, and wants to share exceptional experiences, they will deliver this enthusiasm to others and then those folks will recommend you.

The Experience Elevation Model provides a framework for transforming your client relationships and elevating every aspect of your business. While we've explored each lever sequentially—from enticing attention to igniting advocacy—it's important to understand that these elements don't always operate in a strictly linear fashion. Your journey to creating exceptional experiences may begin at any point in the model, and you'll likely find yourself engaging multiple levers simultaneously as you build deeper relationships with your clients.

The power of this model lies in its flexibility and the various systems you can implement within each lever. Perhaps you'll start by delighting existing clients with personalized touches that anticipate their needs, while simultaneously working to entice new prospects through compelling storytelling. Or maybe you'll focus first on exciting current clients with share-worthy experiences while building systems to invite others into your brand's sphere of influence. The key is to choose the systems and strategies that align with your organization's strengths and your clients' desires.

Remember that each lever offers multiple pathways to elevation. You might incorporate the systems for systematic thoughtfulness, develop your BDA (before, during, after) framework, enhance your questioning techniques, or implement any combination of the tools we've explored. The goal isn't to deploy every system at once, but rather to strategically select and implement those that will most effectively help you build your roster of top-tier clients, differentiate your brand, and create lasting advocates for your business. By thoughtfully applying these systems across the five levers, you will create a comprehensive approach to delivering exceptional experiences that will set you apart in any industry.

CHAMPAGNE MOMENT

Write a handwritten note to someone today and say something nice about how much you appreciate them. If writing notes isn't your thing, send an email. Or if you are on social media, write a recommendation for someone on LinkedIn or a book review for someone on your favorite retailer's website. I promise you, these small actions for you will mean the world to someone else! Easy peasy.

Luxury leaders are continuous learners on a never-ending journey. They inspire teams, influence goals, foster vulnerability, listen deeply, manage conflict, navigate choices, and make tough decisions.

Jennifer Campbell
senior vice president, global events, Virtuoso

Keep Reaching
for Luxury

· · · · ·

Have you ever watched a marathoner cross the finish line? Their face tells a story—determination, grit, and sometimes sheer exhaustion. That moment is the culmination of countless hours of training, solitary long runs, and unwavering focus. It's not easy, but the goal makes every step worth it.

While training for my first marathon, I found strength in an audiobook, *The Unbreakable Human Spirit*. The author's journey from a traumatic accident to marathon training was a testament to resilience. His mantra, "Go a little further, last a little longer, try a little harder, just don't quit," became my own. He reminded me, "Just do it. You'll be glad you did."

That wisdom applies to us all. Whether you lead a global enterprise or run a solo venture, the path to delivering exceptional experiences demands persistence, courage, and a commitment to elevate every interaction.

On this book's cover, you have seen the image of the muselet. When we drink champagne, we must release the muselet, the cage holding in the cork, to enjoy the delicious bubbles inside the bottle. The cork prevents the liquid from spilling out of the bottle; the muselet is its key. Metaphorically, this can represent the things that hold you back from providing exceptional experiences to your clients, to your team, in your personal and professional life. What cages stop you from attracting the clients you want to serve, from being the leader you want to be?

As our journey through this book concludes, I urge you to keep reaching—for luxury, for excellence, for more. Push a little further. You'll be so glad you did.

Dearest gentle reader, or should I say, dearest luxury reader, our journey together through this book has shared secrets of a luxury mindset, and you now know the five luxury levers of the Experience Elevation Model that will help you deliver exceptional experiences to your clients.

You can use the model as a system to attract the attention of the top-tier clients for whom you want your brand to be top of mind (mind share). You also now have the tools to speak their luxury language, differentiate yourself from your competitors, and create advocates for your organization.

That powerful combination always drives revenue (market share).

One of my favorite quotes on leadership is from one of the most highly regarded leaders in the luxury travel industry, Jennifer Campbell, an executive at Virtuoso: "True leaders are continuous learners on a never-ending journey. While they inspire, guide, and influence a team toward shared goals for collective success, they must also foster vulnerability, listen deeply, manage conflict, navigate choices, and make tough decisions." She is so right! Luxury leaders are on a continuous journey too.

Leaders set the standard of everything by modeling behaviors, attitudes, and priorities they want reflected throughout their team and organization. They establish the tone for the culture, shaping how challenges are approached, successes are celebrated, and values are upheld. A leader's mindset cascades through every level, inspiring excellence, fostering collaboration, and creating an environment where individuals feel empowered to deliver their best. It all starts with the leader—it starts with you.

You are responsible for setting the energy in every room you enter. You set up the expectations of what you and your team will deliver. You set the emotional tenor for those around you who look to you as a leader as their role model—that's you!

When I speak with leaders of service-based businesses, they often want to know how to deliver these exceptional experiences that create advocates. Luxury experiences are the ultimate in exceeding expectations, and exceeding expectations builds long-term relationships. That's why my recommendation is to lead at the luxury level—lead with a luxury mindset; become a luxury leader of luxury levers. When you focus on how you communicate, activate, and elevate everything, not only does that achieve the goal, but it also catches attention, differentiates your offerings, and grows your business.

Throughout our conversation together, I've shared resources to help you build a new luxury leadership toolkit to deliver the most exceptional experiences to those around you. With all the champagne moments we have had together, I thought it might be valuable to share information about where you can get even more information.

If you would like to read an executive summary of our luxury mindset research study, or discover your own luxury mindset by taking our luxury mindset self-assessment (it will take you less than five minutes), visit the Luxury Mindset website (luxuryisamindset.com).

Finally, it has been a privilege to be on this journey with you. Here's to all your champagne moments. I hope that we get to sip champagne together one day in real life. You know what would be really fun? Send me a note and let me know which system of elevation appealed to you the most. You might be surprised to learn how many authors love hearing from their readers, and I especially want to know what champagne moment you chose and implemented because we spent time together. Reach out to me at hello@neenjames.com and share your luxury experience because yes, I want to hear them all, and yes, I answer all my emails. When you are sharing on social media, it would be lovely if you could use hashtags #ExceptionalExperiences #ChampagneMoments, so I see your post and can reshare it for you!

Santé! (That's "cheers" in French.)

Grand Cru
(A Fancy Name for Acknowledgments)

· · · · ·

Like the finest champagne houses select their most exceptional grapes for their Grand Cru, these remarkable souls have been my own "Grand Crew"—the essential blend that transformed this book from vision to reality. In these pages, I raise a toast to those who brought their distinctive notes of wisdom, support, and inspiration to create something truly extraordinary.

Clovis Taittinger, managing director of the Taittinger champagne maison, once said, "Champagne is the best way of saying 'I love you' in any language." So let's imagine we are sipping champagne together!

Picture this: a decadent soirée in a luxurious hotel with panoramic views, the finest decor, and the most exquisite rosé champagne—or your favorite non-alcoholic beverage—flowing freely. Surrounded by laughter, warmth, and love, we are celebrating *Exceptional Experiences* coming to life. Welcome to my imaginary book launch party. Please meet the guest list:

This book is here because of you—your love, belief, and inspiration. Each of you has enriched my life in profound ways, and I am endlessly grateful for your part in this journey.

To my incredible clients: If you're reading this, know I'm talking about you. Thank you for trusting me, welcoming me into your corporate family, and letting me share my ideas and energy with you. It's such a privilege to serve you.

Andy: Your unwavering love and patience remind me that I am the most spoiled girl in the world. You are my constant, my everything. Many authors would agree when a book is published, their partner's name should really be on the front cover too! Harley: Your constant need to play hide-and-seek, close my laptop while I'm typing, remind me you need treats every hour, constantly make me laugh—you are the cutest fur baby!

Michael: You are my partner in fabulousness (and ridiculousness) and match my love for Louis Vuitton. Your friendship is a gift that brings joy, laughter, and an abundance of sparkle to my life. I love our adventures. Samuel and Manny—I love you.

Tamsen: My ride-or-die and the godmother of this book! Your daily texts, brilliant insights, boundless love, and perfectly timed interventions carry me through. I couldn't do life—or this book—without you. Forever and always.

Meg: You are the best friend everyone wishes they had. You are the cool mum. You role-model how to authentically navigate the world with humor and grace. You are the keeper of all secrets—I love you enormously. Thank you for holding space for your "crazy, tiny, little Australian"—forever and always.

Candy: You are the world's most adorable baby sister. Your excitement for this book, and your love, constantly reminds me how fortunate I am to have you by my side.

Aunty Carol: My confidence (and cheekiness) is from you! My earliest childhood memories include your gorgeous laughter, the joy you bring into every room you enter, and being inspired that you were always planning your next adventure. Maybe I get my sense of adventure from you too!

Phil: Your generosity in guiding authors (and friends) is unmatched. Thank you for being a beacon of support and kindness to so many people who are fortunate to call you their friend.

Joey: Your enthusiasm for this book, your love of client experience, and your thought leadership in this area is a gift. I value our friendship so much.

T: You, my brilliant one, are adored and admired, and your input has had a deep impact on my life. Thank you for constantly challenging my thinking and helping me see the world differently.

JJ: You reminded me of my fierce strength, always showing up no matter the time zone or continent. Thank you for your unshakable belief in me and the mantras I repeat constantly: You versus You. Last set, best set. Finish Strong. I adore you.

Jen, Sue, and Tif: You are the dream team! Your encouragement, tireless support, and protection of my headspace made this process possible. I'm so grateful for you all and the way you uplifted me every step of the way.

Jen: You, and Louis and Lillibet, have been the best project managers of this book. Thank you for everything.

Pascal and Laurence: *vous êtes magnifiques et je vous aime tous les deux—à plus d'aventures françaises.*

Irene: Our daily therapy walks are a treasure; your friendship makes life lovelier. You are the most exquisite friend and hostess; I learn so much from you.

Lea: You inspire me with your authenticity and dedication. I'm so proud of you and cherish all our "Dancing Queen" moments.

Mike: You are the world's best keynote director, a creative source making the world a more beautiful place, elevating stories everywhere. So much love and appreciation for you.

Jud and Erin: you two are the coolest—I adore you both and our adventures all over the globe—cheers to creating more memories.

Pam: You are the best business coach and cheerleader a girl could dream of. Your encouragement to explore my belief that luxury is a mindset and share it with the world shaped this book into reality.

Nancy: Thank you for being on speed dial and helping me navigate the globe with style, fun, and so many laughs along the way.

Valerie: You are who I want to be when I grow up. I admire the way you travel the world with grace and style and inspire me to constantly elevate everything in life.

Susan: You validated my belief that luxury is a mindset and elevated it with the research insights. Your work is vital to the world and has enriched this book immensely.

Jesse: Your enthusiasm for this project lights up every conversation. Your belief in me has been a gift, and your joy is infectious. You are the best with the most beautiful heart.

Kendra: You elevated all my ideas and gave them life with grace and brilliance. Your talent made this book even more special, and I am forever grateful.

The Page Two team: You all believed in my vision from the first moment and your expertise and passion have transformed this book beyond my wildest dreams. Each time I hold it am reminded of your genius and dedication to every author fortunate to partner with you.

To everyone who has walked this path with me, joining an audience in a ballroom for a keynote, sitting around a boardroom table for strategic planning, taking a Zoom coaching call, agreeing to be interviewed to share your story, or commenting on a social media post—thank you for making this journey so extraordinary.

YOU are my luxury, my joy, and my reason to celebrate.

I interviewed so many legends in luxury, sales, and leadership to create this book for you, and there are many stories I couldn't include (only because of space) and so much wisdom shared by the following list of people that I admire and will always be deeply grateful to: Matthew Upchurch, Roy Collett, Andrea Grisdale, Cynthia Coutu, Tifphanie Hill, Nancy Ebel, Lisa Holland, Gina Lyons, Fred Maahs, Suzanne Shalaby, Mathieu Roland-Billecart, Irene Lee, Nido Qubein, Catherine Ansel, Bruce White, Philippe Hertzberg, Jaime Klein, Claudia Goettig, Mike Ganino, Nicole Carver, Michael Dominguez, Nikki Upshaw, Shawn Johnson, Anita Jensen, Fiona Dalton, Valerie Wilson, Paul Viollis, Michèle Careau, Lauren Thomas Compton, Wendy Davis, Karen Joyce, Tim Mapes, Sally Turner, Ian Altman, Cornelia Samara, Helen Nodland, Renee Vaughn, Ashly Balding, Theo Androus, Brady Sandahl, Rushton Bowen, Kimberly Wetty, Jennifer Jacobs, Kari LaRocco, David Connor, Ashish Sanghrajka, Úna O'Leary, Jennifer Campbell, Christine Judson, Helen McCabe-Young, Michael Londregan, and Caroline Huo.

Sources of Exceptional Experiences

. . . . .

My research into attention and luxury has spanned many years of my career. The most important research contributing to this book is the luxury mindset research with Audience Audit, founded by Susan Baier. You can find the executive summary, and many more helpful resources I consulted while writing this book, by following the link in the QR code. If you would like a copy of the models and frameworks used in this book to share with your team, you can also find them at this website.

I look forward to seeing you there.

photo: KARA BETH PHOTOGRAPHY

About the Author

·····

Neen James focuses relentlessly on how to make people feel seen and heard and is the author of *Folding Time* and *Attention Pays*. She has been named to the Top 30 Leadership Professionals by Global Gurus several years in a row because of her work with companies including Viacom, Comcast, Virtuoso, Four Seasons, and the FBI.

Boundlessly energetic, quick-witted, with powerful strategies for paying attention to what matters, Neen shares how to get more done and create more significant moments at work and home. She engages, educates, entertains, and delivers real-world solutions for your organization, home, and community. Originally from Australia, she lives in Tampa, Florida.

Let's create unforgettable moments together

· · · · ·

Ready to elevate your organization's experiences from ordinary to extraordinary? Whether you're seeking a high-energy keynote that transforms how your team thinks about luxury and attention, or you need strategic consulting to elevate your client experience, I'm here to help you stand out in ways your competitors can't copy.

I've helped some of the most successful global companies and the coolest brands on the planet transform their approach to luxury experiences. Now it's your turn. Connect with me at **neenjames.com** to discover how we can make your brand impossible to ignore.

Looking for results that excel? Let's chat about:

- Keynotes that ignite transformation for your organization
- Strategic coaching and consulting for your leadership team
- Development workshops that elevate team performance

Your exceptional experience starts here.

If you would like to engage with me further, there are several ways to get exclusive access to my work.

Follow me on Instagram: **@neenjames**

Sign up for my newsletter at **neenjames.com**

Book me for a speaking engagement, and learn about other ways to work with me: **hello@neenjames.com**

More Champagne Moments Celebrating
Exceptional Experiences

"Neen's insight that luxury is fundamentally about thoughtful attention rather than price point aligns perfectly with what we've discovered drives success in leadership and client experience. Every leader committed to continuous development and differentiation should consider this essential reading."
Jennifer Campbell, senior vice president, global events, Virtuoso Travel

"True luxury isn't about big and expensive objects, but small and meaningful experiences launched at a psychologically impactful point on the customer journey. *Exceptional Experiences* is a framework that all business leaders can follow that will transform the relationships they have with their customers."
Jay Baer, author of seven books including *The Time to Win*

"Neen has summited the peak of client experience strategy, offering a clear path for organizations that want to rise above their competition. Just as successful expeditions require meticulous planning, attention to detail, and adaptability, Neen demonstrates how exceptional client experiences demand the same level of intentionality and care. This book is essential gear for any leader who understands that reaching the summit isn't about the view—it's about creating an unforgettable journey."
Alison Levine, team captain, first American Women's Everest Expedition

"In a world of faster, easier, and less human, Neen reminds us of the real luxuries of life and delivers the tools required to help businesses reconnect with their primary asset, their people. After all, we all deserve a little more luxury in our lives, and your business holds the potential to deliver it!"
Phil M Jones, creator, Exactly What to Say

"No one in our industry has a deeper understanding of the luxury buyer and mindset than Neen. Coupled with her extensive executive experience in guiding strategy for many companies, this allows her to offer a pragmatic approach that can scale to any organization. The ALHI family will be applying many of these recommendations as Neen has guided us for many years now, at the complexity of the luxury space."
Michael Dominguez, CEO, Associated Luxury Hotels International

"Offering a powerful and practical road map for elevating your business, this book is essential reading for leaders wanting to differentiate their brand and cultivate lasting customer loyalty by making people feel valued. A must read and highly recommended."
Alexander Chetchikov, president, World Luxury Chamber of Commerce

"In a world that seems too often in a race to the bottom, chasing volume and charging toward commoditization, Neen provides inspiration to those architects of the extraordinary. We have relied on her ability to articulate both what works and, of equal importance, why it works as we continue our quest to build our luxury brand equity."
Michael Londregan, senior vice president, global operations, Virtuoso Travel

"Neen delivers extraordinary insight into what truly matters in business today—creating memorable experiences that transform clients into advocates. Her strategic approach mirrors what we've implemented at High Point University, proving that genuine attention to detail and personalized service aren't expenses; they're investments that yield remarkable returns. Leaders who embrace these principles will not merely compete but stand distinctively apart in our increasingly commoditized world. This book will be prescribed reading for our students."

Dr. Nido Qubein, president, High Point University

"In this powerfully actionable book, Neen challenges you to reframe 'luxury' from high-end and hoity-toity to humble and human: the experiences that can shape your business and signal to your customer that you care deeply."

Ann Handley, *Wall Street Journal*–bestselling author, *Everybody Writes*

"Neen makes the luxury mindset feel less like an indulgence and more like a leadership imperative. This book is your blueprint for turning attention into advocacy and champagne problems into champagne moments."

Ron Tite, bestselling author of *Think Do Say*, *The Purpose of Purpose*, and *Everyone's an Artist*

"Neen will change the way you think about luxury forever! In this brilliant book, packed with her trademark energy and charm, Neen shares the formula for elevating average business interactions into meaningful, memorable experiences that will keep customers coming back again and again. Buy copies for everyone on your team!"

Brittany Hodak, keynote speaker; author, *Creating Superfans*

"Neen has me thinking like a concierge to develop the kind of connection with my clients that creates unforgettable moments worth remembering. It's time to stop settling for satisfied customers and start creating passionate advocates."
Brant Menswar, author, *Black Sheep* and *Designing Momentum*

"Creating memorable experiences isn't about grand gestures or massive budgets—it's about the thoughtful attention to those little things that make all the difference. Neen's model and five luxury levers can be implemented by any company and align with what today's leaders know to be true: customer satisfaction is rarely about price or product, but rather how the experience makes people feel. Essential reading for leaders who understand that in today's crowded marketplace, customer experience is your most powerful—and cost-effective—marketing strategy."
Dan Gingiss, keynote speaker; author, *The Experience Maker*

"Neen's approach to luxury isn't about extravagance but making people feel valued through personalized attention and thoughtful service—something that you can easily weave into your sales process. I've witnessed how her strategies help organizations dramatically improve client retention and referrals by creating memorable moments that drive revenue."
Ian Altman, bestselling author, *Same Side Selling*

"People don't remember transactions—they remember how you made them feel. Neen nails the formula for crafting experiences that excite, delight, and ignite real loyalty. This is a must-read for anyone who wants to create fans for life."
Jesse Cole, owner, Savannah Bananas; founder, Banana Ball

"The last competitive edge in building your business: help buyers feel special and feel seen. Neen has found a way for you to systematize that advantage. Appropriately, it's exceptional!"
Jay Acunzo, author, *Break the Wheel*; storytelling strategist

"Neen's approach in defining luxury based on how our clients perceive luxury was transformational for me. I now realize a luxurious experience can be analogous to upping your game or being better every day so that your clients AND team members feel special. I highly recommend this book!"
Jennifer Addabbo, CEO and cofounder, Engage fi

"Everyone desires luxury; few understand how to deliver it. Neen is one of the rare individuals with the knowledge, experience, talent, and skill to turn everyday interactions into a series of memorable moments. Revealing the secrets of luxury brands worldwide, her strategies will work for everyone from the solopreneur to the global enterprise. You'll learn how businesses at the pinnacle of luxury create the remarkable interactions to keep their clientele coming back for more."
Joey Coleman, international keynote speaker; *Wall Street Journal*–bestselling author, *Never Lose a Customer Again*

"Neen has hit the bull's-eye on how to build an exceptional brand. This book is a master class in aligning experience with your brand promise, using all the senses. If you follow Neen's advice, you will ignite raving fans who will tell others and grow your business."
Dr. Jim Schleckser, bestselling author, *Great CEOs Are Lazy*

"*Exceptional Experiences* shares how to tactically convert traditional everyday transactions and make them unique, memorable moments. Neen shows you how to make the experience your brand provides your single biggest competitive advantage."
John R. DiJulius III, bestselling author, *The Customer Service Revolution*

"Experience is no longer a luxury. It's an absolute necessity. Service is the price of entry, but delight and crafting extraordinary experiences are how to thrive in the Age of AI. Neen is a master of that. For decades, she has been making delight, excellence, luxury, and brilliance the heart of what she does."
Matt Church, founder, Thought Leaders Business School

"As someone whose business is built on deepening relationships, Neen's luxury approach is invaluable for creating meaningful connections and memorable moments that our CADRE members rave about. Whether I'm playing trusted advisor, rolling out the red carpet for new members, or empowering our top-tier clients to become our welcome committee, her framework provides practical systems for bringing personal attention and concierge-level service to everything we do!"
Melanie Coburn, cofounder and chief relationship officer, CADRE

"Neen reminds us that luxury isn't about price tags—it's about how you make people feel. *Exceptional Experiences* is a master class in creating moments that matter, led by someone who knows how to turn attention into lasting loyalty. Every leader serious about growth and relationships should have this on their desk."
Michael Barber, chief marketing officer, StarTech.com

"Reading *Exceptional Experiences* feels like sipping champagne with the sharpest, most stylish strategist in the room—and Neen is exactly that. This book flips the script on what 'luxury' means in business. It's not about price—it's about presence, personalization, and performance. Neen gives you a front-row seat to a world where being intentional, paying attention, and crafting standout client moments becomes your unfair advantage. If you want your brand to feel like first-class storytelling on a private jet, start here."
Mike Ganino, #1 bestselling author, *Make a Scene*; public speaking and communication director

"No one designs, lives, and breathes luxury like Neen. *Exceptional Experiences* will help you differentiate your brand, increase revenue from existing clients, and bring more beauty, joy, and connection to your work."
Pamela Slim, author, *Body of Work* and *The Widest Net*

"In today's hyper-competitive marketplace, customer loyalty is the gold standard. Your business needs more customers who become your advocates in the marketplace. But that will never happen if all you do is what you've done. That's why Neen's distinctive new book is your new manual for profit and success. She will teach you how to take your organization from where you are to where you want to be."
Scott McKain, author, *ICONIC*

"Neen delivers a master class on elevating business interactions from ordinary to truly unforgettable. Having witnessed her strategies transform our organization first-hand, I can attest that her luxury principles create meaningful results that directly impact the bottom line. Her practical systems provide leaders with immediately actionable tools to create advocates, not just customers, which is the true path to sustainable growth."

Shannon Lofdahl, founder and principal, Navin Collaborative

"Neen created a playbook for turning everyday customer interactions into remarkable experiences worth talking about! If you want to create the kind of amazing experiences that keep customers coming back and telling others about you, this book is a must-read!"

Shep Hyken, customer service/CX expert; *New York Times*–bestselling author, *The Amazement Revolution*

"In *Exceptional Experiences*, Neen reframes luxury as a mindset accessible to every business, not just high-end brands. Her systematic model delivers exactly what change leaders need. What makes this work so powerful is how Neen combines rigorous research with practical implementation strategies that honor the way humans actually experience change and connection. If you want to drive meaningful transformation in how your organization creates client experiences—and measurable results in revenue—this is the road map you've been waiting for."

Tamsen Webster, founder and chief learning officer, Message Design Institute